CHARLES S. TOGIAS

A GREAT "HOW TO" BUSINESS BOOK!

CREATE LOYAL CU$TOMER$ IN AN UNLOYAL WORLD

A step by step "How to" create a dynamic customer focused business.

Copyright © 2009 Charles S. Togias
All rights reserved.

ISBN: 1-4392-5348-X
ISBN-13: 9781439253489

Visit www.booksurge.com to order additional copies.

Acknowledgements

I want to thank Nick Phillips, a great actuary turned editor for his wise advice and tireless dedication in the editing of my book.

I want to thank Rudy DuBay for his computer knowledge and attention to detail.

And of course to my wife who endured my many long hours in the writing of my book with her usual style, patience and grace.

PREFACE

I am a leadership, sales, and marketing consultant and own a company called Step2 Training Systems. **Create Loyal Customers in an Unloyal World** is my third book, and it is very unique for two reasons. First the title is also the name of my seminars,' and second, it describes in detail every element of my Step2 Training System. It is so complete with the "how to" it could be read by a college professor and taught at a university. My system is dynamic yet simple and if implemented properly would help any business succeed.

My experience was in radio broadcast advertising, where I first implemented many of these elements with great success. There is no theory in my system, and it has been tested in the field with great results. When I was general sales manager for an AM/FM radio station in upstate New York, our leadership and sales team grew to be the largest revenue sharing stations in the country.

Every element of my system is in proper order to insure maximum effectiveness. To build a customer focused corporate philosophy, you must articulate your focus and then develop a strategy to accomplish your goal. The philosophy section includes a Corporate Mission Statement, Core Values, and a defined Competitive Edge Identity. All of these elements are clearly explained in my book and after reading **Create Loyal Customers in an Unloyal World,** you and your staff will find it very easy to develop.

To create a successful corporate philosophy, it must be employee driven. Your employees are the key to your success, and they should be involved in every aspect of your customer focused system. If a corporate philosophy is solely dictated by the managers, it will fail. Take time in the hiring process, and only hire people with great attitudes with a willingness to learn. You need the right people to implement a successful customer focused culture.

Leadership training includes: defining the leader's role, 15 steps to successful leadership, how to develop a leadership, clarity of purpose statement, and more. All clearly explained for easy implementation.

Since my background is sales leadership, the employee section of my book is invaluable. Employee productivity will increase, and a new team spirit will emerge. I stress employee participation in all aspects of the system in order to insure success. When employees help develop the system they take ownership, which insures a positive outcome.

Preface

You will notice in the table of contents and in the upcoming chapters that leadership, staff training and sales training have similar elements such as: added values, standards and disciplines and personal marketing resumes. This is very important to assure that everyone is properly trained in the new customer focused philosophy. I want to reiterate that all employees and all departments must be involved in the development of the corporate philosophy.

My book even includes a marketing section that is also invaluable. I will show your company how to develop a marketing model designed to narrowly focus on the heavy users of your goods and services. The model defines your target, their key buying considerations and how to create a positioning statement.

There is also included an actual Job Description/Evaluation Form, Personal Marketing Resume, Client Needs Analysis, Leadership Statement and a Departmental Plan. All completed in detail for your easy understanding. In addition I included my Step2 Training workbook that was developed to reinforce the system for those that took part in its creation and it is great for training new recruits.

To summarize my book I equate my Step2 Training System to building a house. The employee is the architect, the leader is the builder and the blue prints are supplied by the system. The bricks and mortar represent the mission, core values, standards and disciplines, personal marketing resumes and more.

If you own a business and want to build a more successful corporation, my book is for you. Many corporations have implemented the techniques found in my book and have distinguished themselves very favorably among their client's. I hope my book is of great help to you and the success of your company.

• • •

Table of Contents

I. Corporate Philosophy 1
    A. Corporate Mission Statement 17
    B. Core Values 25
    C. Competitive Edge 29

II. Leadership 35
    A. Defining a Leaders Role 39
    B. 15 Steps to Successful Leadership 45
    C. Leadership Clarity of Purpose
       Statement 49
    D. Standards & Disciplines 53
    E. Personal Marketing Resumes 55
    F. Brainstorming Techniques 59
    G. Monitoring the New
       Customer Focused System 63

III. Staff Training 65
    A. Departmental Added Values 67
    B. Standards & Disciplines 71
    C. Personal Marketing Resumes 75
    D. Creative Problem Solving Meetings ... 77

IV. Sales Training 79
    A. Sales Added Values 83
    B. Standards & Disciplines 87
    C. Personnel Marketing Resumes 91
    D. Client Needs Analysis 99
    E. Techniques & Terminology 113

1. Buying modes 114
2. Buying cycle 115
3. Buying influences 115
4. Client Needs Analysis vs. Budget 117
5. Recommendation vs. Choice 119
6. Written Presentations 120
7. Creative Problem Solving Meetings 122
   F. Strategic Account List Management 125
   1. Ideal Customer Profile 127

V. Marketing 131
   A. Marketing Model 135
   B. Positioning Statement 139
   C. Strategic & Tactical Campaigns 143

VI. Administrative
   A. Customer Focused Job Descriptions 146
   B. Departmental Plans 155
   C. Training Workbook 158

Epilogue 171

Client Quotes 175

Authors Bio 181

CHAPTER 1
Corporate Philosophy

I believe that in order to insure a successful outcome you must have a strategic plan. Sun Tzu the famous Chinese general once said "It is that in war, that the victorious strategist only seeks battle after victory has been won." He felt the planning for the battle was climactic and the battle itself was anti-climactic if the plan was executed properly. When developing your corporate philosophy, you create a focus and then develop a strategy to accomplish your goal. The more unique and customer focused you become, the more successful you will be.

Step2 Training Systems has a very simple corporate philosophy. You can create loyal customers only if your entire company is trained in techniques designed to delight your customers beyond industry standards. Creating loyal customers will insure increased revenue and market share. It will also make competitive attacks very difficult.

To create a customer focus culture, you give your customers value in their purchases accompanied by exceptional service (we are going to focus on exceptional service in this chapter). It is a very simple philosophy, and in my book I will explain in detail each element needed to achieve success.

Focus all your attention on super serving your customers and your revenue share will increase. For a customer focused philosophy to be effective, everyone from the CEO to hourly employees must be immersed in the implementation and training process. I want to reiterate that to be effective all employees must have a say in its development and then given the autonomy to execute without corporate limitations. This will require strong effective leadership with a dedication of purpose. Leaders that are confident and willing to share their power with their staff in the development of the corporate philosophy is a testament to their leadership.

Most companies rely on product and price as their competitive advantage. This is a problem because products can be easily compared and price is the weakest marketing position a company can have. All a competitor has to do to attack a price position is lower their price. A customer focused philosophy with every employee dedicated to creating loyal customers is your true competitive advantage.

The more creative the customer focused environment becomes, the more difficult it is for a competitive attack. The goal of the company should be to become the industry leader in customer loyalty. Employee input and autonomy is the key to the success of your corporate philosophy.

Corporate Philosophy

Employees are the key element because when employees are involved in the creation of the philosophy, it insures consistent execution. When employees can claim ownership they are more willing to participate. Development and dictates of a philosophy, only inspired by management without employee input rarely works. I cannot stress this fact enough.

Hiring the right people is always a challenge but especially so in a customer focused environment. Attitude should be at the top of your requirement list. There is an old saying "That you can't win the Kentucky derby on a jack ass," no matter who the trainer is or what you feed them. It is also true that you cannot create a customer focused philosophy, when you employ the wrong people. I've always felt as a sales manager that I could train almost anyone in proper sales techniques. It is much more difficult to change an employee with a bad or questionable attitude. It takes years to develop your attitudes and it may take years to change them. Don't waste your time.

In my leadership sessions, I have always said that if an employee fails, it is usually their manager's fault. The manager either hired the wrong person or trained that individual incorrectly. Take time in selecting your staff, because your success will be determined by the growth of each employee.

People focus is an important key to a successful organization and most companies are not aware of it. Some years ago I was training a car dealership in proper customer focused techniques and I was challenged by one of the sales managers. That day he had a confrontation with a customer and wanted my opinion. In fact he said that because I was not in the car business I did not understand how unreasonable customers could be. The customer in question came into the dealership and wanted the dealer to replace his windshield wiper blades on his two and a half year old car at no cost. An argument ensued, and the customer left in a rage. He said that he tried to explain to the customer that he was being unreasonable because no windshield wiper manufacturer in the country will warrant their product for 2 years. The customer would not listen and left. He then asked me what I would have done.

Before I answered I told him I needed to get some information. I asked him if he had any information regarding; when the average person trades in their car for a new car, and he said traditionally every 3-4 years. Remember the customer that he had the confrontation with had a two and a half year old car. I asked him how much did your irate customer's car cost new and he said $21,000. I then asked him how much does the dealership have to pay for windshield wiper blades and he said $6.00. I said you lost a $21,000 asset for $6.00. Isn't that insane? He said positively not.

I went on to answer his question by saying that I would let the customer know that no windshield

Corporate Philosophy

wiper manufacturer in the country warrants their product for 2 years but I not only will install the windshield wiper blades I would like him to wait a few minutes so I could have his car washed. The sales manager then replied I was opening a can of worms because what if everyone wanted the dealership to perform this service. I said if that happens, get on your hands and knees and thank God because you will be able to effectively position your dealership as very special in your targets mind for $6.00 per customer. What a great opportunity. The sales manager found out as the sessions went on that he was not really in the car business he was in the people business.

When I was a general sales manager in the broadcast industry, I would always help my employees understand that their success was reflected by their client's success. There was a quote that we use to have on our office wall. "We will never ask for your business unless we can help improve it." My staff needed to let their clients know very quickly that they were there to solve problems and grow businesses. We lived by those words and in our sales meetings we would always review client successes and effective strategies.

We were dedicated to exceeding our client's needs by identifying our client's problems and then developing a strategy to solve those problems. Our primary job was to help our clients achieve success through our strategic recommendations. Many times we would help our clients in areas not related to radio and did not reap a financial benefit for ourselves, but it did wonders for our reputation.

Our dedicated customer focused sales professionals would conduct a client needs analysis to uncover business opportunities for our clients, whether or not it involved using our radio station. One such case involved a franchise dealer with American International, who wanted to end their relationship because of an on going disagreement. The owner of the company, Pat Tucci, wanted to drop the franchise, but was concerned because he did not want to lose his identity with his customers. He was in desperate need of a name change. Pat called me and asked for our help. I gathered a group from our radio station to conduct a brainstorming meeting to help rename the company, keeping in mind that our goal was to rename the company without confusing his customer. Within two hours, we renamed the company and solved our customer's dilemma. The name we came up with was Americar. The name Americar allowed Pat to drop the American International franchise and remain in business without confusing his customers-goal accomplished. Pat sent me a clock inscribed as follows: "With our deepest appreciation the mangers and sales reps of American International 1990." I still have the clock and cherish it to this day. This problem had nothing to do with selling advertising, and everything to do with helping our customers succeed.

Corporate Philosophy

I was once in Rochester, New York and was introduced to a broadcast sales manager that was highly thought of in his industry. During our discussion, I asked him what was his number one job priority and he answered: "to maximize inventory for my radio station." He then asked me the same question and I said "to get results for my client." He said to me that we shared a different philosophy and I thought to myself thank goodness. By the way he was in a larger market and our billing revenue significantly exceeded his company's revenue.

I learned that when you solve customer problems, which lead to their ultimate growth it insures customer loyalty. It creates a win-win situation. As you help your client's grow you grow. When all employees in your organization strive to achieve goals and objectives consistent with its Mission and Values the workplace becomes very dynamic. My Step2 Training System will never become outdated because it focuses on the success of each customer. It was my philosophy when I was in the broadcast business and later refined with my Step2 Training System. Most broadcast companies that sell advertising use a different philosophy, and that is why, in my opinion, most of them do not maximize their revenue potential.

Instead of uncovering client needs, broadcast companies have a cost per point selling philosophy. They have an industry focused mentality. They do not uncover client needs, instead they tell their clients how many people listen to their station. They subscribe to various rating services because their largest source of revenue are advertising agencies and they buy almost exclusively cost per point. Their need to satisfy ad agencies has caused bad habits.

These rating services gain their listener information by phone interviews or by in home diaries. When completed they will determine the listening habits of various age groups. This sounds good in theory, but the information is flawed. The numbers are weighted, which means a small number of participants in the survey will determine the listening habits of a much larger number of people. I was much more interested in the psychographics of my listeners than in the weighted, inaccurate numbers.

Are the listeners rich or poor? Do they live in the city or suburbs? Do they reside or work close to my client's place of business? Do they need the product being offered? Who are they and what programs attract them to our radio station?

Step2 Training Systems philosophy deals in logic and reality. The marketing concepts of the Step2 System, encourages our clients to follow a different process when trying to market their product from the standard advertising philosophy. This will become very clear in the marketing section of my book.

If you ask most companies if they are customer focused they will always reply "yes." Most com-

Corporate Philosophy

panies feel that a customer focused philosophy is merely being courteous to your customers. They rarely encourage employee input when formulating the philosophy and almost never give employee autonomy. Their corporate policies will be filled with what the company can't do to satisfy the customer. Remember great companies are not trained to satisfy their customers, they train employees to delight them. There is a huge difference between the two. You cannot delight your customers when you formulate a long list of can't do's.

For example, most companies have many stipulations on returned merchandise and in doing so run the great risk of losing their customers. Within the last year, I was involved in such a situation. Around nine months ago, I purchased an air compressor to fill our bicycle tires. We rarely used the product as we have limited our bike riding in favor of walking. I used it a total of four to five times and the last time I used it, it broke.

I purchased the compressor from a store called Tuesday Morning in Naples, Florida. Tuesday Morning is a discount chain that sells various products. I paid $10.00 for the product. When I went to return the product, without a receipt, I was told it was against corporate policy to accept an item without a receipt.

Obviously, I wrote a letter to the corporate offices to voice my concerns. I look at these situations under a magnifying glass because of the

Create Loyal Customers in an Unloyal World

business that I am in and wanted to inform the company about its unfriendly and unprofitable corporate policies. The letter is as follows:

Tuesday Morning
Customer Service
Att: Shaniqua
6250 LBJ Freeway
Dallas Texas 75240

Within the last year I purchased an auto air compressor (#AC12/4481) from your Tuesday Morning store in Naples, Florida. The item cost $9.99. I bought the item to fill my bicycle tires and it was used very infrequently. I paid cash for the item and did not keep my receipt. A couple of weeks ago I tried to use the air compressor to fill my tires and it broke. So I attempted to return the item and was told I could not do so without my receipt. I was told by your manager that it was against company policy to return any item without a receipt.

I own a company that does customer focused training to include creating a corporate customer focused philosophy, leadership, sales and marketing training. My company, Step2 Training Systems has helped companies as far away as Australia in proper customer focused techniques. Losing a customer over $10.00 is insane.

I can certainly afford losing $10.00 but your company can ill afford to lose a customer for life. To survive in today's

Corporate Philosophy

competitive world a company must do everything possible to grow their customer base. When you visualize how much of a marketing effort it takes to secure one customer you must also visualize how to keep them.

Creating customer focused: Mission Statements, Core Values, Positioning Statements, employee training and marketing are my expertise and when I see an organization participating in dangerous practices I want to call it to their attention. A word to the wise is usually sufficient.

I hope you take this criticism as constructive and it serves to improve your bottom line. I always urge companies to listen to their customers after all the customers are the ones that will grow your business.

Sincerely,
Charles S. Togias
CEO Step2 Training Systems

I wrote the letter to help the company understand that their policies may be preventing them from delighting their customers. I do not care about the compressor as I have a bicycle pump to replace the one that broke. I was more interested in their response. Unfortunately, I have yet to receive a response.

Contrast that type of corporate philosophy with Publix, a super market chain with several locations in the Naples Florida area. In fact, they have one location that is in the same shopping center as Tuesday Morning, but Publix has a completely different way of doing business. It's my understanding that Publix's policy complies with a 100% satisfaction guarantee with no questions asked, because I have never had a problem returning anything with or without a receipt. Every employee that I have encountered at Publix is always ready to assist the customer by solving the problem, and they do not have to ask the manager for permission. It is a pleasure to shop at Publix.

I started my sales career in broadcast advertising and worked for 24 years in the industry before starting my leadership, sales and marketing consulting company Step2 Training Systems. I had great success as a general sales manager at WSYR AM/FM in Syracuse, New York, with a station that previously had a continual decline in revenue.

In 1978 I was named sales manager and inherited a 17% revenue share in a 21 station market. By 1982 we grew to a 40% revenue share and because of our growth potential we were purchased by a New York City firm Katz Communications. Katz Communications was lead by some very creative and aggressive broadcasters out of Fairfield. Connecticut.

In 1983, they changed our FM format from rock to adult contemporary and hired more staff. We brought in an FM sales manager to help with our tremendous growth. By 1986 our team had

Corporate Philosophy

amassed a 55% revenue share, and we dominated our Central New York market. To understand the dominance that meant that our two radio stations took 55% of all the dollars spent in radio, while the other 19 stations shared 45% of the total market. We ranked #1 in share of revenue in a medium to large market in the USA.

In summary, to formulate a customer focused corporate philosophy you must do the following:

1. Gather management and selective staff from different departments and discuss all the elements needed to create a unique customer focused philosophy. Do not follow or be concerned about current industry standards. In fact encourage everyone to think out of the box and try to implement policies that far exceed traditional corporate behavior. The more dynamic and unique the policies are in delighting the customer the more effective it will be in favorably positioning your company among their many competitors.

2. Once you have formulated the philosophy, invite all departments to evaluate it and encourage all employees to give suggestions on how to make it even

better. The philosophy will come alive when all employees have ownership.

3. Hire employees with great attitudes. Employee autonomy is an important key to the success of your new customer focused culture. If employees are trained correctly, they should not have to ask managers when it comes to delighting the customer. Employees will build strong customer relationships and loyalty when the customer understands that the employee has the power to solve their problems without management restrictions.

4. Corporate policies should be short and to the point. Do whatever it takes to delight the customer.

I understand that it is not always possible to delight every customer. I also know that it may be accomplished more easily if companies would only be more customer focused. Look at every customer as a long term investment when evaluating the problem. Losing a long term asset over nickels and dimes is just foolish. Don't be penny wise and pound foolish.

In a customer focused culture, the word no should be eliminated as a first response to a customer request. When asked a question by a customer, instead of replying "no" all employees

Corporate Philosophy

should respond by saying "let me try to find a way to help." Remember that old saying "I don't care how much you know till I know how much you care."

• • •

A.

Corporate Mission Statement

"Clarity of Focus assures execution"
Charles S. Togias

In formulating a corporate philosophy the first element is to create a customer focused Mission Statement. It is the start of creating a corporate identity and is a very important element in becoming customer focused. Your Mission Statement will bring clarity of purpose to everyone in your organization. Especially when it is created with employee input.

In the past, many companies have formulated Corporate Mission Statements and have completed them in error. One of the reasons for this may be that only senior management was involved in the process. If you are formulating a customer focused corporate philosophy, who is better qualified to assist in this process than the employees who interact most closely with the customers?

It has been my experience that a Corporate Mission Statement is one of the most important, yet one of the most confusing, elements of the entire process. When created by management, most Mission Statements become too long with a confusing message. They have a tendency to describe too much, and therefore have little value to the corporation. I have seen Mission

Statements that were two pages long, and no one in the company could articulate its meaning. Complexity leads to ineffectiveness.

In this chapter we are going to discuss what a Mission Statement is, who it is focused on, how to formulate one, and how to make it come alive. I love simplicity and clarity of message because I think the world is complex enough without me adding to the confusion.

What is a Mission Statement?

A Mission Statement is nothing more than a number one job priority. In a customer focused company, your Mission Statement revolves around super serving your customer. Everything else is secondary. It is a rallying cry that unites all employees and departments with a single purpose. Your Mission Statement becomes your corporate identity.

Who are your customers?

Your customers are basically three groups. **First,** they are the clients who purchase your goods and services. **Second,** they are your peers, those individuals that work within your corporation. It is impossible to become a customer focused organization when there is unresolved employee strife within your company. As Abe Lincoln said: "A house divided against itself, cannot stand".

Corporate Philosophy

Corporate unity is one of the main reasons why I include employee input when creating the system. To create a special dynamic environment, everyone within your organization must work together for a common cause. **Third,** they are your vendors, those individuals that supply your company with needed supplies to help increase your productivity. When you are good to them they will return the favor.

I am going to use sports and politics to make my point and emphasize the importance of working together. Athletic teams understand and embrace their mission while politicians in Washington, DC are confused. The most successful sport franchises strive for team unity and spirit. They have one goal-team victory. Their focus is to formulate a well thought out game plan designed to assure victory. Everyone works together and takes responsibility for the goal to be achieved. Sport's teams understand their mission and know the only way to accomplish it is through team unity.

The Republicans and Democrats, on the other hand, are an example of a house divide against themselves. They are elected by the people, and they should have a common, united goal to bring prosperity to those who elected them. Once elected both parties should be working together and no longer be rivals. The problem is that both parties hate each other and want each other to fail.

Instead of working together as a team with a united goal to make America great, they do the opposite, because they have lost their sense of purpose. Their mission is self serving, and therefore internally focused, and we as Americans are paying the price. There is an old saying that describes the outcome that can be expected from this type of leadership- "when the elephants fight the ants take a hell of a beating." Since our politicians are not united with a defined mission, we are getting the hell beat out of us.

I wanted to illustrate the negative effects our two party system is having on America to emphasize how important it is to have a united purpose. Your Mission Statement must have a single focus that all employees embrace to be dynamic. Everyone must identify who they serve and how they serve them.

How to implement?

When formulating your corporate Mission Statement, you must gather management and selected employees. All employees will have their eventual input, but in larger companies it is all but impossible to include everyone in the initial process. A facilitator will be selected to lead the meeting by writing down management and employee suggestions. The questions that need to be addressed are the following: Who are our customers? What is our company's number one job priority?

Our customers, as we discussed previously are our clients, peers and vendors. The list can also include stockholders and any person or group deemed as important by the group. The second question defining your number one job priority will be focused on meeting and exceeding your customer needs. I always include the word enthusiasm in every Mission Statement I help create. When you perform any job with enthusiasm you take customer focus to a new level.

How to make it come alive?

When your initial Mission Statement is completed, it will be shared with all other employees that were not involved in the process to be fine tuned. Employee input is vital in the Step2 process, and it is very important to have everyone take ownership.

Once the final Mission Statement is completed, management will quiz their employees on their understanding of the statement, and how they are implementing it on a daily basis. Employees will know that their job evaluation requires them to live the statement. When employees understand that they are required to know the statement verbatim, and are also being judge on their ability to perform the statement, it will come alive.

Recently, I helped my friends in the Small Business Development Center (SBDC) at Florida Gulf Coast University create a Mission Statement for their department, and also had the pleasure in assisting another company Riebesell Chiropractic Center in the formulation of its statement. I will show you both statements and the reasoning behind the message.

The Small Business Development Center's number one job responsibility is to help small businesses succeed by providing professional business advice. I wanted to assist them in creating a statement that gave them a narrow focus while helping to create team unity. The statement is as follows:

"WE ARE A CUSTOMER DRIVEN ORGANIZATION OF BUSINESS PROFESSIONALS, DEDICATED TO HELPING SMALL BUSINESSES SUCCEED, BY ENTHUSIASTICALLY PROVIDING CREATIVE SOLUTIONS WHICH EXCEED CUSTOMER, EMPLOYEE AND STAKEHOLDER'S EXPECTATIONS."

It is a powerful statement, because it narrowly defines the organizations number one job priority. Also when your corporate identity is defined clearly with everyone's input that will create team unity. I believe a Mission Statement to be effective must be clear and concise. A wordy confusing Statement is worthless. Keep in mind that more is less and less is more.

Dr. Riebesell of Riebesell Chiropractic Center wanted me to help him create a clear identity

Corporate Philosophy

and a dedication of purpose for him and his staff. He supplied a list of what he and his staff though were most important to his patients when coming to his medical center for treatment. To paraphrase the list, his patients wanted professional medical treatment to insure their health and well being in an environment that was courteous and respectful. The statement created was as follows:

WE ARE A DEDICATED STAFF OF MEDICAL PROFESSIONALS ENTHUSIASTICALLY COMMITTED TO THE HEALTH AND WELL BEING OF EACH OF OUR VALUED PATIENTS, BY PROVIDING SUPERIOR CHIROPRATIC TECHNIQUES IN A KIND PATIENT FRIENDLY ENVIRONMENT.

This statement also narrowly defines the chiropractic centers most important job responsibility. It will give the entire staff a clear vision on what is expected of them. There is no confusion as to their role in creating delighted patients. Both statements are powerful in their simplicity.

• • •

B.

Core Values

Core Values is the second element needed in establishing a dynamic customer focused ideology. I believe a successful company must create a set of important values that are beneficial to their customers, all their customers- internal and external. These values once created will be posted in the different meeting areas, and be a guide to the decision making process. Great companies are similar to the functional family; they will not compromise their integrity.

Before I discuss Core Values pertaining to business, I want to digress a bit. I have always been fascinated why some families are normal and functional, and other families are in complete disarray. They could live in the same block and have similar backgrounds. They could enjoy the same standard of living, yet one family is functional and productive and the other is not.

Because I spent many years helping companies create a corporate philosophy I think I understand some of the reasons why and they are the same reasons for businesses being in disarray. The functional family is lead and influenced by strong adult leaders, who are dedicated to the families continued growth and development. Everyone within the family is required to follow a set of rules designed to bring unity and tranquility. Those rules were created by the adult influence and carefully explained to the rest of the family as to their importance. Everyone was required to take responsibility for their actions, and they were disciplined when necessary. I believe strong discipline designed to help children improve is a show of love. I feel the same way when management disciplines for the purpose of growth.

I believe that the functional family is the model that is most responsible for the child becoming a successful adult. When I was working in the radio broadcast business, our company hired a group out of Lincoln Nebraska called SRI. SRI was a company that did employee interviews to determine the sales or management aptitude of current employees or those seeking employment.

I came from a functional family with a very strong non-compromising father and a loving dedicated mother. It was a great combination. When I was tested by SRI, I had never read a management book in my life, and yet scored in the top five percent in the country for my aptitude in management. They said that I instinctively understood the techniques of successful management. The more I thought about it, the more I was convinced that the functional family is the purest form

Corporate Philosophy

of personal development. My in home training as a young child was invaluable.

When you develop a set of Core Values, you are creating a successful environment. You are creating a functional business family. Corporations that encourage these business practices demonstrate to its employees that they care. Since I believe that the functional family is the greatest model a corporation can emulate, I am always enthusiastic to implement these very important values.

When I am involved in creating these values I focus on three important areas:

1. Outstanding Customer Service

2. Employee Training and Autonomy

3. Corporate Honesty and Integrity

These values are employee driven. The following is just an example on how they may read:

1. **Our dedicated employees will continually strive to delight each customer by implementing outstanding industry leading customer service.**

2. **Our employees are our most valuable asset, and their continued development will reflect our corporate dedication.**

Their ability to solve our customer problems are the reason for our success.

3. **Corporate and individual Honesty and Integrity at all times.**

These are examples of creating corporate Core Values. Every company will create its own set of values to be determined with employee input. It's the same scenario, a group of managers and employees will formulate these values, and then each department will review and fine tune if necessary. Once they are created, Core Values are never compromised. The implementation of these values will help your company become functional.

• • •

C.

Competitive Edge Identity

When creating a corporate philosophy, I believe that each element should be clearly defined. Your defined Mission Statement will give the corporation a corporate identity. Your Core Values will give internal guidance and inspiration, especially when they are both designed and created with employee input. Creating a corporate identity and guidance within your organization is vital when formulating a corporate culture. It helps your entire company understand their united role in the company's success.

When I do my seminars, I always start off by asking the same two questions. Both questions are closely related to each other. My first question is: Why should I do business with your company? Followed by: I am thinking of doing business with your company, how does it benefit me to do business with you? They are easy questions, yet most people I have encountered have trouble answering them.

The answer to the first question would be to articulate your corporate Mission Statement. Your Statement was designed to give your company a corporate identity, and if it does not it should be changed. Many companies have a Mission Statement, and they just may not realize that it gives its corporation an identity. When this happens, I question the process they went through to develop it. Remember when all employees in your company helped design the statement, can articulate the statement and are required to give examples on how they live it day to day, the statement becomes your corporate identity.

But what about the second question: How does it benefit the perspective client to do business with you? If you are in sales, you are asked that question every day on every call, and most sales people do not realize the question when it is being asked. Just as your corporation needs an identity, so does each individual within that organization.

My system is different because it goes beyond helping corporations achieve an identity. I also focus on the people, who are most responsible for creating and implementing that identity. That is why I am so adamant on employee involvement. Everyone within the organization from the CEO to the floor sweeper should understand their role in your company's success. Your true competitive edge is your people, and they need to fully understand their importance. Each individual in a dynamic customer focused organization is vital to the success of the company, one is not more important than the other.

Corporate Philosophy

Since your competitive edge identity is each employee, it should be focused and revolve around each one of them as individuals. In other words when I help employees create their competitive edge identity it will give all of them an individual identity. To do this I make sure that every statement that I facilitate always starts with the word "me." This reminds each employee that they have to take responsibility for the desired outcome.

I noticed something many years ago when I was a sales manager that really concerned me. I found that most salespeople were identified with the product they sold and as a result they unconsciously removed themselves from the sales equation. They allowed their product and price to be their identity and that is a problem. If you are identified with anything other than your ability to solve problems, you have no identity, your product does. When this happens price will become the determining factor in your success. A customer focused philosophy understands that its people and their ability to solve problems is the company's competitive edge.

There are too many businesses that allow their employees to pass the buck. They practice what I call "the hot potato mentality." When a customer is in need, they pass them on to someone else as fast as possible. When your employee driven Competitive Edge identity starts with the word me, you have to take responsibility for the outcome.

Remember when employees help formulate their Competitive Edge Identity, they will own it and must take responsibility for its success.

The next word or words I like to include in the development of our statement revolves around being empathic to each customer. When you demonstrate empathy you exhibit the ability to understand the character, perspective, and values of your customers and peers. Employee empathy is paramount in a customer focused culture.

I like employees to be knowledgeable. To use their expertise so I always try to include industry knowledge or expertise when designing the identity statement. It forces the employee to take responsibility for the desired outcome.

To be a valuable resource to your customers, you must focus on your ability to solve problems. So I always encourage my clients to include words like "problem solving" in their defined competitive edge identity statement. If you are a problem solver, you become a valuable resource; if not, you are of little significance.

When I facilitate your competitive edge identity statement it will revolve around answering the question: How does it benefit me to do business with you? Your Competitive Edge identity will answer that question, and may sound something like this: You should do business with me because of **Me, My Empathy, My Expertise and My Total Dedication to Solving Problems.** The statement

Corporate Philosophy

means that the individual is taking complete responsibility for a successful outcome by being empathetic to you and your situation, using their knowledge with an ultimate goal of resolution. That is a great reason to do business with anyone and it is a powerful identity.

The identity statement answers the question, and gives everyone in your organization an identity and responsibility for a successful outcome. Your competitive edge identity statement will give all employees a customer focus that will reinforce your corporate philosophy. An identity statement designed correctly will give all employees a strong personal conviction about themselves, and provide a strong attachment to the corporate philosophy. Each individual will become more confident, convincing, and persuasive, which will be beneficial to the company and its customers. One statement designed correctly will give an identity to all and be beneficial to every customer.

• • •

CHAPTER II

Leadership

"Successful leaders define expectations and monitor results in a caring, disciplined environment"
Charles S. Togias

Once the corporate philosophy has been established the responsibility for its execution lies with management. Strong effective leadership must provide an environment that assures its proper implementation. Establishing a philosophy and actually living that philosophy can only be accomplished with dedicated leadership. They must involve all employees and have an uncompromising dedication of purpose.

Vince Lombardi was quoted as saying "Leaders are made, they are not born; and they are made just like everything else has ever been made in this country-by hard effort. And that's the price that we all have to pay to achieve that goal or any goal." I agree with him 100%. Leadership is instilled at an early age, and it starts in the functional home as I stated earlier. It takes a lot of effort to develop strong leadership qualities.

Great leaders all have one thing in common: they improve on the behavior of people. That is how effective leadership should be measured-on the improvement of people's behavior. Whether it is in the home, school or workplace great leaders move people in the right direction. The qualities they demonstrate are discipline, communication skills, consistency, taking responsibility for their actions, enthusiastic praise for a job well done, and attention to detail. They lead by example, and leaders never ask those they lead to do anything that they wouldn't do themselves. Leaders never make excuses for their failures and have an attitude of "if it is to be, it is up to me." Leaders are an inspiration to all.

Unfortunately we have others that disguise themselves as leaders, who have a different focus. I refer to them as fake leaders, and you can always identify them because they are always blaming others for their lack of progress. We see this with our politicians in Washington that are always blaming the other party for their inefficiencies. Community Leader's, who's communities, have been in disarray under their leadership for many years resulting in stagnation. They always blame others for their lack of process, and characterize those in their communities as victims. I agree that those in these unfortunate communities are victims, because they have to endure this type of leadership. That's why I always have said that great leaders improve the lives of those they lead, and fake leaders stagnate the lives of those they mislead

When you take and encourage others to take responsibility for their actions that is leadership 101. Leaders lead by example and are always willing to admit their mistakes. Real leaders judge their

Leadership

ability with one criterion in mind: are those they lead improving their skills and behavior? Are they better employees, citizens, family members etc?

In this leadership chapter I review and define the qualities that make great effective leaders in business. I define these qualities, step by step, and introduce a very simply and easy formula that anyone can follow. If you adopt these simple suggestions, it will enable you to perform at a very capable level.

Always take into consideration one very important element when you are in charge of leading others. You must do what you say, and say what you do. You will lose credibility if you do otherwise. An example: If both you and your employees create a list of good standards and disciplines, which we will do in this chapter, you must live by them. Your leadership position requires you to be the role model. If you do not, your employees will lose respect for you and your ideals.

A customer focused culture cannot exist without strong dynamic leadership. This chapter will give you the knowledge to become a compelling leader. I feel very confident that when you adopt these leadership principles, you will become a strong and more effective force within your organization. Remember judge your own performance by those you lead and their continued ability to perform at an increased level.

• • •

A.

Defining a Leaders Role

"Successful leaders improve the skills and behavior of those they lead. Everything else is secondary."
Charles S. Togias

In my leadership seminars I ask my attendees to narrowly define their role and most important job responsibilities. I want them to focus on areas that will be most beneficial for those they lead. I want them to concentrate on the skills that are most important to the individual, department and company, in that order. Individual growth guarantees department growth, and department growth guarantees corporate growth. So if every individual is trained properly to maximize their effectiveness, everyone benefits.

Businesses must be outcome focused and sales driven to survive in today's competitive workplace. Someone that leads a department will be judged on their ability to maximize the output of that department. To do this a leader must understand effective leadership.

The role of a leader is to establish the conditions under which all employees will chose to execute the mission and core values of the company. In order to accomplish this, a leader must be insightful, trustworthy, dedicated and empathetic.

A leader's five most important responsibilities are as follows: to lead, to develop, to motivate, to discipline non-performance and to formulate strategy.

Leaders Lead by "defining expectation and monitoring results in a caring disciplined environment." With the input of staff, the effective leader will create and define good performance and monitor everyone in their ability to execute. Defining good performance is important when monitoring staff. It insures good performance and improving performance is the definition of leadership. Leaders are role models always walking the walk is how they earn respect. Leaders understand that they have to command respect and not demand it. When they make a mistake they address it head on, meet with staff and find a new direction. They involve their staff in all department policies. They lead by example.

Leaders are always **Training** and **Developing** their staff. The training never stops. The staff will meet at least once a week to discuss in field successes and failures. The successes are important as they serve as a guide to good performance. It stimulates thought and helps others when formulating a strategic plan for their clients. The failures are as important, as they demonstrate what does not work and what is needed for improvement. Staff is encouraged and assigned to train other staff members. Example: If a new employee was hired in sales, I would assign the previous hire to participate in the training. It would accomplish a couple of goals. First, it would bring the employees together and help in our team building. Second, it helps the employee that is conducting the training to better understand the product and philosophy behind it. When employees are required to train, they know they have to be well prepared. I involved every employee in some part of our new employee training program.

Most business people would convey to me that it was impossible to **Motivate** staff in the business arena; obviously, this is non-sense. I believe the carrot without the stick is useless, as well as the stick without the carrot. Leaders must acknowledge and reward good performance to encourage their employees to repeat that performance.

This is very evident in sports. We see an athlete score a touchdown, and all his teammates will rejoice and shower him with praise, and that is a great lesson for us in business to understand. It is important because it does three things that are also important in business. First, it clearly describes what good performance looks like; second it creates team unity when everyone rejoices for their teammates; third, the celebration is so joyous it energizes other team members to score so they can be recognized, and that is always good. Don Clifton said "there is no success without celebration." Effective leaders must discipline so they may celebrate success.

Acknowledging good performance is vital to a healthy customer focused environment, and **Disciplining Non-Performance** is just as important. All employees must know that there is a standard of excellence in your organization. Employees will never improve unless their errors are identified and corrected. We have reiterated many times in this book that leaders improve the lives of those they lead, and if that is true they must discipline and correct those that are not performing. How else will they improve?

When I was interviewed by SRI regarding my aptitude for management I remember one question in particular. They asked me; how I would handle an employee that would not follow the rules of the department? When this happens it is an attitude problem more than a lack of understanding in regard to sales techniques, and I have very little tolerance for people with bad attitudes. So I answered the question by telling the interviewer that I would tell the employee that their actions are detrimental and causing a morale problem among staff members. Soon after, the interviewer hypothetically asked what I would do if I approached this employee again, and the employee still would not respond. I told the interviewer to go on to the next question, because I cannot identify with her assumption. She asked me why not, and I said that I would explain it to the employee only once and not twice. The first time would be a warning from me and the second approach would be the pink slip.

Leaders discipline to improve behavior and productivity. They will never allow one employee to destroy the team. If you are afraid to discipline non-performance, leadership is not for you.

Leadership

Sun Tzu said "the general who wins in battle makes many calculations in his temple before the battle is fought." The main reason there is call reluctance in sales is the fear of failure. Most sales people are well versed in their product and understand industry specific data. They are much less prepared in understanding how to formulate a well thought out **Strategy** designed to lessen client resistance.

Information is the most important element when building a strategy. JFK said, "Every man made problem has a man made solution." When dealing with our clients, we would gather as much information as possible through a client needs analysis, and review the information with our team prior to meeting with our client. We would examine the need, review their competitive situation and plan a successful strategy. When you do enough of these sessions in a group environment, the team starts to become one. Our strategic planning solves our customer's problem and increases our ability to think strategically in the field.

If you are currently a manager and want to become a highly respected leader, embrace the elements that we have just discussed. Leaders lead by example, develop and train, motivate through recognition, discipline non-performance, and formulate strategy.

• • •

B.

15 Steps to Successful Leadership

These 15 Steps to Successful Leadership are very simply to embrace and dynamic when implemented.

1. Always conduct your business beyond reproach.
   - Never ever lie to employees or clients.
   - Be a role model. Do what you say and say what you do.

2. Always evaluate employees on a consistent basis.
   - Recognize each client's success so your employees will be able to repeat their performance.
   - Help identify and manage weaknesses so your employees can improve.

3. Never show employee favoritism
   - Every employee should abide by department policies and standards.
   - The principles on which to manage an army are to set one standard of

courage that all men must meet. (Sun Tzu)

4. Always respond in a timely manner to employee requests and problems.
   - Treat your employee concerns as if they were your concerns.
   - Let your team know that you care.

5. Always formulate clear expectations with employees.
   - Clearly define what you expect from every employee.
   - Get employee input when defining job responsibilities.

6. Always keep a line of communications open.
   - Encourage employees to discuss job-related subjects
   - Always make time available for employee strategic client discussions

7. Always stress employee involvement.
   - Encourage your employees to participate in the day to day activities involving your department.
   - Involve all employees in the training of new staff.

8. Always stress employee empowerment.

Leadership

- When employees are properly trained, give them the authority to make it happen.
- Employees must have autonomy to build customer relationships.

9. Always encourage creative thinking.
    - Every employee should be encouraged to think as an added value problemsolver.
    - Create an employee recognition award for the most creative client solutions.

10. Always make people development your #1 job responsibility.
    - Every person in your department is a reflection on your ability to lead.
    - Conduct strategic weekly departmental meetings with staff.

11. Always celebrate success through employee recognition
    - "There is no success without celebration." Don Clifton
    - Consistently recognize good performance.

12. Always discipline non-performance.
    - When there is no discipline the standard of excellence will decline.

- Discipline is the key to a functional environment.

13. Always demonstrate a "can do" attitude and find a way to help.
    - Build a positive team environment
    - Encourage and promote team unity

14. Always make decisions in a timely manner.
    - Companies that over analyze are rarely market leaders
    - "Cleverness has never been associated with long delays" (Sun Tzu)

15. Always be a strategist preparing your team to succeed.
    - Plans and strategies should be formulated in the office, not in the field
    - The general who wins in battle makes many calculations in his temple before the battle is fought. (Sun Tzu)

My 15 Steps to Successful Leadership is a guide and should be referred to as often as necessary. It has been very helpful to me and my clients. As your skills and knowledge increase you may want to add to or revise the list. This is just a guide in helping to focus on effective leadership.

• • •

C.

Leadership Clarity of Purpose Statement

In this section of my book, a clarity of leadership statement, in as few words as possible, is developed by management. Their statement will be similar to a mission statement, but only focused on leadership. This is a very important exercise for leaders, as it keeps them focused on their most important priority- their people. I do this because no matter how much I stress employee development to management, they seem to always get side tracked on different projects. I realize there is more to management than people development but everything else that they are engaged in is trivial in comparison.

The most important elements in effective leadership (refer to prior section) needed to be discussed prior to developing the statement. Managers must realize that they exhibit true leadership when those they lead become successful through their guidance. Everyone in the organization should understand the vital role the leaders play in the success of the corporation. When we formulate job descriptions later in the book, we will prioritize all duties for every department. If leaders are bogged down with trivial non people development duties, I strongly suggest that they delegate those responsibilities to non management staff.

Non development responsibilities for corporate leaders are similar to sports. Having leaders focus on these non productive duties is like having the New York Yankees management requiring A-Rod to miss batting practice, to sell hot dogs. The franchise has to make money with the sale of hot dogs but they would be misguided to have A-Rod selling them. That type of management I call a robbing Peter to pay Paul mentality.

Managers become leaders when the employees they manage improve all of their skills. I cannot stress this fact enough. Even when I do, some senior executives in corporations insist that non development duties are required by management and maybe they are but they are not a priority for leaders. If productivity drops it can be attributed, many times, to a lack of direction in leadership within the corporation.

I go back and forth using the term manager and leaders, because I try to clearly communicate the difference between the two. Managers supervise departments and leaders develop people. If your corporation is going to grow, your employees must continually improve their skills. Employees improving their skills and behavior through effective leadership is my definition of leadership.

Leadership

Hopefully I have stressed this point so let's move on with the formulation of the statement. Formulating a leadership clarity of purpose statement is very similar to a mission statement. It clarifies, and is a constant reminder to leaders as to their #1 job priority. We gather our managers (they are not leaders yet) in a room and ask them the same two questions: Who are your customers and what is your number one job priority? Their customers are those that work for them. Their number one job priority, if you don't already know it, is to continually develop and cultivate their staff in order to maximize work performance.

Recently I got permission from a company I did business with some years ago to use its actual leadership priority statement in my book. The company is Ontario Credit, which is an equipment leasing and finance company. They hired me to create a customer focused philosophy that included leadership, employee and administrative training. The owner of the company is Mr. Louis Centolella. I worked very closely with him and his son Louis Centolella III.

Louis III was an example of a dedicated manager that had great potential to become an effective leader. It has been my experience that second generation family members are usually the most difficult to train, as many of them feel they have entitlement. Louis was the exact opposite and was a very willing participant in the training process. His growth as a leader was outstanding; as a result, his company flourished. Louis and I have remained great friends to this day, as I have the upmost respect for him.

To develop the statement, we gathered department heads with a few of the company's top employees and clearly defined the manager's most important job responsibilities. When developing these statements, our focus remains very narrow. Our goal is to develop a simple yet powerful statement that defines a leader's role, and keeps them focused on that role. The statement we came up with is as follows:

"To Achieve Our Mission by Empowering my Team of Highly Dedicated Problem Solvers, Focusing on being the Best Leader, the Best Listener, the Best Motivator and the Best Teacher That I can possibly be."

The statement focuses the leader to create a team of problem solvers. To accomplish this, the leader must be the best listener, the best motivator, and the best teacher. It is a powerful statement, and it is general enough yet specific enough to be used by all of the department heads/leaders in the company. Louis Centolella III has become a great leader, because he lives this document daily. The statement will only come alive when it is executed on a continual basis.

• • •

D.

Standards & Disciplines (Leaders)

To ensure a customer focused philosophy, the corporation must have a defined set of standards & disciplines for everyone to follow. All departments must be involved in there development. Each department will determine what rules and regulation are needed to assure good performance. The corporate statements are worthless unless they are accompanied by an employee and department specific list of standards designed to improve the culture. Without these specific standards & disciplines leaders cannot hold their employees to a high standard.

When creating these standards, every employee in the department must have input. It is an important part of helping to continually give a structure to the new culture. Once it is created, it will allow leaders to monitor good performance, and since all employees in the department were involved in creating these standards, there should never be any surprises. To expect good performance, you must carefully define and articulate a set of standards and disciplines. To insure its execution, your employees must help to create it.

You cannot live your corporate mission statement without the help of your entire staff.

Willie Sutton was a famous bank robber and when they asked Willie why he robbed banks he replied: "Because that's where the money is." But he said something else I like even better, because it draws a parallel to what he said and having a Mission Statement without a way to monitor it through a list of standards & disciplines. Willie said, "That a kind word and a gun will always get you more than just a kind word." Willie was a smart man, because the corporate Mission Statement is the kind words, and the Standards & Disciplines are the gun. The kind words are worthless without the gun.

Each department will create their own standards & disciplines specific to their own needs. The department leader will facilitate these meetings. The leader will also create their list, which will focus on various areas such as: How to conduct a professional stimulating meeting. This will include having a defined itinerary for every meeting, dated action plan for follow up, specific start and end times (professionals are never late) etc. Whatever department leaders feel is important in creating a professional environment will be included. Whatever ends up on the list cannot be compromised.

• • •

E.

Personal Marketing Resumes (Leaders)

Personal Marketing Resumes (PMR) are one of the most effective elements that I have created for companies. Those individuals that have used them properly have achieved great success. The PMR is a one sheet handout designed to position the employee as a valuable, added value problem solver to their target audience. When presented correctly, it will position you and your organization effectively in your target's mind. It is not only a great leadership and sales tool, it is a marketing weapon and will reposition your competitors for not having one. It positions your competitors as unprofessional and not ready or committed to do business.

The department leaders PMR will differ from sales because their primary target is different. When sales design's their PMR, they will focus on their clients, those that do business with the company. The department leader will focus on those they lead and perspective employees. Both will become very effective positioning tools. The personal marketing resume will very clearly describe what the customer should expect when doing business with you and your company. It is a very special positioning tool.

My book and each training element should be followed in the order that I have presented. I recommend that the leader's PMR session start after defining leadership, a leader's role, clarity of purpose statement, and standards & disciplines for maximum effectiveness. Each element is presented in this order to effectively support the other. It is similar to constructing a building. You need a strong foundation before adding floors.

When interviewing potential new employees, I would hand them my leadership PMR. I would say to them that if they accepted a position with our company, this is what they could expect from me. The first item they would see is my manager's mission statement, which I would explain. Then they would see a list of my commitments regarding the training and development of staff. At the end of my PMR, they would see my phone numbers and email address. I said phone numbers, plural, because it is preceded by the statement available 24 hours a day 7 days a week. If you are not accessible to your customers, you are not customer focused.

The PMR can be effectively created from the leader's mission statement. Here is an example:

Leadership

Name: Louis Centolella III, Leader and Developer, Sales

My Mission: To achieve our mission by empowering my team of highly dedicated problem solvers, focusing on being the best leader, the best listener, the best motivator and the best teacher that I can possibly be.

My Commitment to you:

To build a team environment with a one for all and all for one attitude

To provide strategic weekly training sessions and infield training

To define the importance of requested projects

To provide the necessary materials to do your job

To recognize and praise top performance

To provide a dedicated support staff committed to quality work

To provide an environment for continued growth

To clearly define expectation and monitor your results

To care about you as a person
Available 24/7/ 365
Work#
Cell#
Email#

If you were interviewing for a job/career and one leader handed you this PMR and the other "manager" did not, who would you think was more professional? If you are seeking a job you may not care, but if you are seeking a worthwhile career, the leader displaying the PMR wins.

The PMR when created must not be compromised. Your reputation is most important in your personal and business life. When you create a PMR you are accountable to live by what you profess.

. . .

F.

Brainstorming Techniques

We keep stressing the fact that having a Customers focused philosophy requires you and your company to become a team of added value, problem solvers. To become this unique type of resource, you need to be able to access many creative ideas. Your entire organization has to have the capability to create an idea bank. Great customer focused companies are never standing still. Those companies are always looking for new ways to improve itself and those they serve.

In sales I have always said that the finest sales people that I have ever encountered rarely sell product at a price, instead they recommend problem solving ideas. Customer focused companies become an invaluable resource to itself and its customers when they look beyond traditional methods of doing business. Information stimulates thought and thought stimulates creative ideas. Creative ideas stimulate corporate and individual growth.

Brainstorming is a very important element in being able to bring forth ideas. The process is easy and when the rules of brainstorming are followed, the results may be very beneficial. When the process is understood, it may be performed as many times as needed. I am going to review the techniques of brainstorming. These techniques were given to our broadcast company many years ago, and they are still relevant. Over the years, I have tried to simplify the process as much as possible.

Brainstorming has an assigned facilitator and specific rules, and the rules must be strictly adhered to. There are four rules for an organized brainstorming session. Rule1: There is no initial judgment of ideas. Every idea is written down. Rule2: Everyone in the session is of equal rank. Rule3: Encourage wacky and wild ideas. Rule4: The more ideas the better. The initial purpose is quantity, quantity, quantity.

The facilitator in all brainstorming sessions serves as the scribe. The problem is stated in this manner: In what ways might we (IWWMW), and then state the problem. The goal of the session is to develop an action plan with creative ideas designed to solve the problem.

The first session is to gather as many ideas as possible. You are just trying to generate lots and lots of ideas; the wilder the idea the better as we previously stated. All ideas must be written down; if they are not, they are being judged. In this session, you are trying to inspire thought among the participants.

The second session is to evaluate those ideas, and therefore, in this session all ideas are judged.

Leadership

All logical ideas are kept for the next phase. The ideas without value are crossed out and discarded.

The third session is to combine ideas. In this session, two or more ideas are combined to again inspire thought and a solution to the stated problem. The goal of this session is to create an action plan. The final decision and direction is left up to the person who is in charge of the session. The one in charge with the final say is the one who organized the brainstorming session to assist their client.

Great companies are always trying to think out of the box. The goal is to become industry leaders setting the standard of excellence not following it. Organized brainstorming is a great way to generate a limitless number of ideas.

• • •

G.

Monitoring: The New Customer Focused System (Leaders)

"Leaders define expectations and monitor results in a caring disciplined environment." That is my own quote, and I have used it many times in explaining what defines good leadership. A corporate culture must be monitored to be successful. Every element of the system must be closely monitored to insure its execution.

A mission statement is powerful when all employees in the company embrace it by implementing it daily. It is the leader's job to ensure its execution. Creating the system is worthless without daily monitoring. It would be like teaching someone the fundamentals of hitting a baseball, and then never having them swing the bat. The system becomes credible when it is being implemented and fine tuned.

I recommend framing and hanging the Corporate Mission, Core Values and Competitive Edge statements in every room, where employees hold their meetings. When the meeting ends they should evaluate the decisions they made versus their new corporate philosophy. The two must coordinate and support each other. The most destructive thing a company can do is claim a philosophy, and not live it.

Leaders in each department should meet with their staff individually, and review how the staff implemented their defined Competitive Edge Identity. When the employees know that they will be continually evaluated on their execution, they will start to understand that the new philosophy is real.

Leaders should also be continually evaluated. After they have completed the leadership elements of the training, they should be quizzed on how they are implementing those elements on a daily basis. The success of the philosophy depends on all employees' ability to execute it.

· · ·

CHAPTER III

Staff Training

Now that the leaders have been trained in the proper techniques of our new customer focused philosophy all employees must follow, by being completely immersed in the process. With the help of their department leaders they all must create a new team environment. The success of the company depends on everyone's dedication and commitment to the process.

I keep stressing the importance of employee involvement in a customer focused organization. All employees must be trained and monitored in order for the philosophy/culture to become successful. I cannot stress this point enough, because there are some organizations that try to prioritize employees as to their corporate value. I know that some departments contribute more to the bottom line than others, but all departments are designed to support each other.

Sales would have a difficult time competing without the help of their support staff. Employees that type the letters and answer phone calls of irate customers are a great asset to any organization. Employees that service the equipment after it has been sold, working closely with the customer to fix problems that prevent a loss in productivity, are also invaluable. The accounting staff that insures proper disbursement of the corporation's funds and even the cleaning staff that makes the office a nice place to work are all very valuable to a functional organization. They all are important and they need to be properly recognized.

Recognition for a job well done is the leader's responsibility. In sales it is not difficult to offer recognition, because salespeople get a report card every month in the way of a commission check. Other departments are not so lucky. Employee day to day duties may become mundane, and their lack of enthusiasm for their job can jeopardize the organization's performance.

This chapter demonstrates how to avoid employee lack of enthusiasm from happening. We will discuss and formulate a list of departmental added values designed to bring a special incentive to employee's work discipline. We will define a list of standards & disciplines to assure clarity of performance for each employee. Every employee will also formulate their individual PMR' to create a new sense of pride. We will complete the training by structuring a way to measure and improve their performance in the establishment of weekly creative problem solving meetings. These meetings will be a weekly review, monitoring the effectiveness of our training.

• • •

A.

Departmental Added Values (Staff)

Every employee in every department in the organization has to understand how their performance affect's the entire company. Most companies have job descriptions, defining the specific duties required for each employee. Those job requirements are rarely exceeded, and the department continues to function in a traditional way. The jobs usually become mundane, and the employees working in those jobs become disinterested.

The problem with most job descriptions is they are usually formulated by management without employee input and rarely, if ever, updated. Employees that have been in their job position for a long period of time may have gained great insight as to a better way of performing. If management doesn't interact with its employees to get their input, productivity will suffer.

Another problem is that most job descriptions are never reviewed with the employee. In most companies, employee job descriptions are given to employees at date of hire with no future changes or updates. We will discuss more about how to maximize job descriptions in the administrative chapter of my book.

An important part of my customer focused philosophy is to create a culture that exceeds the industries highest standards. This philosophy can be realized only when employees are encouraged to strive beyond their comfort zone. This is accomplished when department leaders encourage their staff to brainstorm ways of increasing productivity through added value techniques.

Added values are what an individual, department, or organization can do above and beyond the normal working requirements. As an example, when you are having your car serviced at an automobile dealership, the technician is required to do the designated service work, nothing more and nothing less. The dealership does not want any extra work done for the customer; in fact, most dealers frown upon it.

That is why there is very little difference in most car dealerships. And that is also why price is the most important factor in the selection of an automobile at a dealership. Those dealerships that have done business differently have effectively positioned themselves as a valuable resource.

What if the service department decided to change its mindset and started to give their customers added value services. To effectively do this, they would have to gather all their service

Staff Training

employees and have them brainstorm those services. They would then establish a list and monitor its effectiveness. They may also obtain valuable input from selective customers.

The added values may include simple things like washing every car inside and out after it has been serviced. It may include something more unique like having a service vehicle that travels to different locations to provide free service, such as charging a customer's dead battery. If you were stranded on the highway, this is an added value service that you would really appreciate. The more unique the list the more impact you will have with your customers.

To insure its uniqueness, the dealership may also have each mechanic formulate a PMR. The mechanic would have the PMR stapled to the invoice to let the customer know, who worked on their car. This would accomplish two things, and they are both very positive. First, it would reposition all other car dealerships for not having this added value service. Second, the mechanic would feel a great sense of pride for a job well done, because they would have to take responsibility for their work. I guarantee you that it would improve the mechanic's job performance.

When you decide to formulate and implement these added values, you meet weekly. The initial week is to establish the values, and the following weeks are to review its effectiveness. You will be able to judge the effectiveness of these meetings by how much excitement the added values have created internally. As more meetings occur, more added values will be recommended.

• • •

B.

Standards & Disciplines (Staff)

Just as we did with the department leaders, we have to do with all departments. We have to establish a clearly defined set of standards & disciplines. Employees cannot be recognized for following the rules or disciplined for breaking the rules, if there are no set rules.

In my employee training sessions, many times employees would show up late. I would never call them to task on it before we established standards & disciplines. After the list was established; if they were late, I would call them aside and remind them that they helped established these standards. In other words these standards & disciplines were not my established standards & disciplines, but they were created and owned by them.

In each meeting it was stressed to the group that the newly created customer focused philosophy was never to be compromised, especially something as important as standards & disciplines. You are trying to change and improve your culture not defend it.

When you pick a facilitator, it should be someone who is strongly convicted to the new culture without being dictatorial. I will always encourage discussion, but would not compromise customer focused values. In other words, I would not let the group replace a customer focused value for something mundane.

Standards & Disciplines should always include respectful and professional behavior. All departments should include punctuality in its list. Along with proper attire and respect for their fellow employees. Profanity should never be allowed in a customer focused organization.

Many years ago we had a nationally known speaker, who will remain nameless, come to our radio station. I invited him to speak at our sales meeting, and that was a big mistake. His language was insulting, especially to our female salespeople. One of our female salespeople took him to task on his conduct, and I didn't blame her. She gave it to him with both barrels.

I called the meeting short and met with him alone after the meeting. He tried to justify his actions by saying that my salespeople were adults, and he was treating them as such. I told him he was wrong, and in our meetings, we never talk to each other using profanity. He felt very uncomfortable and learned a hard lesson. The lesson I learned is that you will never insult anyone by not using profanity, but you may insult someone if you do.

Staff Training

Professional organizations must act professional. Your standards & discipline should reflect your respectful behavior. You should always treat everyone with dignity and respect.

• • •

C.

Personal Marketing Resumes (Staff)

Personal marketing resumes for everyone is a great way to make your people accountable and raise their standard of excellence. We do not have to repeat how to create a PMR because we have already done so in the leadership chapter, but I do want to stress its importance for all departments.

They are a wonderful sales weapon, and companies realize it as soon as I demonstrate its importance. They are a great positioning tool, and salespeople must constantly position themselves to be unique. I never have to explain their value to sales departments, it is recognized immediately.

PMRs for support staff or other department's is a harder sell. Companies feel that they have to only worry about its external competitors. I feel that personal marketing resumes are very effective internally as well. They bring a sense of pride in workmanship to the organization.

When an employee develops their personal marketing resume, they have created a high standard for themselves and feel obligated to perform at that level. Making the PMR creator accountable is the most powerful reason to develop one. It's your choice!

• • •

D.

Creative Problem Solving Sessions (Staff)

I have discussed with you the importance of monitoring my system once it has been formulated. Creative problem solving sessions are designed to insure execution. Each week a scheduled meeting will be set to review the new customer focused culture.

Each department will schedule their own meetings and will have a detailed report on the progress they are making. They will discuss areas of concern and make recommendations designed to alleviate the problem. They will also discuss the areas where the most progress has been made. The meetings are designed to have the new culture become standard operating procedure.

On a monthly basis all department heads and designated employees will meet to discuss ways to create a closer unity among departments. An action plan will also be formulated and reviewed at the following meeting. These meetings should have a start and end time, and are not meant to be work intensive. The meetings are meant to update each department on the progress of the philosophy.

• • •

CHAPTER IV

Sales Training

The training of the sales department in the new philosophy is the most important element in assuring a successful corporate outcome. That is because the salespeople have a profound affect on those people inside and outside the company. They have to demonstrate their dedication to the philosophy with everyone, peers and clients alike. It will be evident to all who interact with sales, if the new culture is real.

In today's competitive marketplace being a sales driven company is more important now than ever. Sales driven companies are instinctually customer focused for two reasons. First, they have to deal with customer's everyday; second, they derive their income from the customer. Sales driven companies understand a very important rule, they cannot stay in business if they ignore or upset its customer base. If you're smart you never bite the hand that feeds you.

When I am asked to help a company become more customer focused and they are sales driven, the transition is half way there, they just need structure. When a company is product focused, it is a much harder transition. It has been my experience that the companies that are the most difficult to convert to this philosophy are companies that are engineering focused.

The reason for this is engineering and sales are diametrically opposed to each other. Engineering is an exact science, and sales' is more of an art, a chart and graph thing versus a people thing. I had the experience of trying to change an engineering group to a sales driven company and was unsuccessful. The owner wanted to change but kept reverting back to what he knew best. The company unfortunately, is no longer in business.

Being sales driven is actually much more advantageous to your customers than being product focused. That's because smart sales driven companies are focused on its client's success and not just interested in selling them a product. When their clients grow their sales increase; it is a win-win situation.

There are only two ways you grow in business. First, maintain and continually grow the accounts you have, and second, you find new accounts. That is why I say when a company starts to lose customers for trivial reasons, you better re-examine your policies. If you are not careful, you may be committing corporate suicide. It is very important when you read this book that you are honest with yourselves. You will not reap the benefits of my book, if you are not willing to change your thought process, if necessary.

Sales Training

I mentioned earlier in the book how cumbersome return policies can eventually affect your bottom line, and that is because the people that create these policies usually have little to no aptitude for sales. They are corporate pencil pushers that are so interested in the bottom line, it confuses their thought process. Nothing affects the bottom worse than a dissatisfied customer.

In this chapter we are going to discuss customer focused sales elements. These are field tested techniques that will help any organization succeed. They will never be out dated, because they focus on the customer and their continued growth. In fact as I said my entire system is obsolete proof. My system and my sales techniques will always be relevant and on the cutting edge.

Later in this chapter I am going to introduce you to one of the finest sales reps in the country- Alan Peck. I met Alan many years ago and had the pleasure of training him. I am going to give you his history and his accomplishments. I am going to show you his current PMR. I introduced the PMR concept to Alan in 1993 when he was employed by Copytronics in Orlando, Florida.

I hope you get a lot of useful information in this chapter. My customers frequently tell me that the best thing they like about my training is that it was relevant and can be implemented the next day. That is the best compliment I can receive.

• • •

A.

Added Values (Sales)

Added values are what you do for the customer above and beyond product and price. When formulating added values for sales departments, you must be very creative and unique. Even companies that do not have a customer focused philosophy have sales reps that are very creative in customer focused techniques. I indicated earlier that sales reps understand that their income is based on customer loyalty and survival is wonderful because it forces people to get creative.

The difference between a sales rep from a customer focused philosophy, and a sales rep that has the misfortune of not benefiting from that philosophy is the quality and uniqueness of the added values. Giving customer's added value services will be appreciated, but unless they provide real value to the customer's business, the added value services will eventually become mundane. Wining and dining a customer is always nice and may reap some benefits, but customer's need to continually improve their business techniques in order to survive. Supplying tickets to sporting events is always a welcomed gesture, but unfortunately everyone can play that game.

A customer focused rep from a customer focused philosophy has added values that are so important and so unique to the customer that when they are implemented, it will effectively reposition all other competitors. These dynamic added values I am referring to are in your new customer focused philosophy. Just as I mentioned earlier in the book, my staff and I facilitated the name change for a company. When we did this, I not only became a very important member of his staff, my staff and I repositioned all the other media competitors as insignificant.

When your entire corporation is immersed in a customer focused philosophy, the philosophy becomes your unique competitive advantage. If your customer needs a corporate identity, who is better qualified to help them formulate a Mission Statement? Your corporate identity was formulated with employee input, and if you were not part of that exercise, someone on your team was. That also applies to your defined Core Values and Competitive Edge Identity. If you were facilitating the development and implementation of this very important corporate philosophy change for your customer, you would become very special to them. Effective sales techniques is a game of positioning, and when you become a real added value resource to your customer, you and your company will own the marketplace.

You could also facilitate the development of Standards & Disciplines, Added Values and PMR's all of which would dramatically help your customers business and cement your relationship with them. Another very important thing happens when you bring this type of value to your customer, you effectively position yourself with all the buying influences within the organization. This is very important, and we will discuss this in more detail when we come to the buying influence elements later in this chapter.

Added values will help you develop strong relationships with your customers. Make sure that you work very diligently at delivering added values that are unique and beneficial to your customers. If you take the customer focused added values that we just reviewed and expand on them, I will assure you that your customers will find them very valuable. No matter what product you are selling, your ability to position yourself and your company as an added value resource will pay great dividends.

• • •

B.

Standards & Disciplines (Sales)

The customer focused sales department has to look more professional and respond to its clients differently from all of their competitors in the marketplace. To do this, they must gather as a group and describe what constitutes outstanding performance. They should discuss industry standards and view them as average operating procedure (AOP), always focusing on being the industry innovator.

When I am conducting my training sessions for companies, I would invariably have someone tell me how the industry does it. When I hear the reply, I always respond to them by saying "so what." Knowing industry standards is only important if you want to follow them. They are of little importance to an innovated customer focused company. If you are true to your culture, you are setting industry standards not following them.

I found this out the hard way. I came home from Viet Nam in 1968 and almost immediately started to sell radio advertising. I was never trained in any techniques other than knowing my product. We were required to wear a suit and tie and given a rate card. Most media sales reps were irresponsible regarding timeliness and usually late for in office and client meetings. The atmosphere was lax, to say the least, and I was learning some bad habits.

One day, early in my career, I made a call to a jewelry store to solicit advertising and was ten minutes late for the appointment. I introduced myself and started to introduce the benefits of my radio station. I got about three words out, and the customer interrupted me and said "How dare you come to this appointment late." I tried to apologize, and he proceeded to throw me out of his office. I was devastated.

At first, I was embarrassed then I got angry. When I had time to reflect, I knew that I was wrong, and the customer was completely justified for his outrage. He was giving me his valuable time, and I took advantage of it. It taught me a valuable lesson that I have never forgotten. In fact, it was because of that incident that I created defined Standards & Disciplines at my radio station when I was promoted to sales manager and currently use them to this day.

As in the development of all the other elements of the system, your department gathers as a group, with a facilitator, and has an open discussion on this topic. Everyone in the group participates, and the facilitator encourages the group to make a list that is unique and very customer focused.

Sales Training

Here are some of the S&D I have helped companies formulate:

1. Phone calls-all morning calls are returned before going to lunch, all afternoon phone calls returned before leaving for home.

2. Meetings with clients or staff must have a defined itinerary with start and end times, with the goal of creating an action plan (we do not want to waste our client's time).

3. Punctuality is always the rule with all meetings (never compromised).

4. No drinking of any alcohol during business hours.

The list can go on; I just recommend that you do not make it so long that it becomes confusing. The facilitator will discuss the list with department leaders after it has been formulated for their input and suggestions. When completed, the list should reflect a disciplined department with a professional code of conduct. Leaders must monitor their employees to assure each S&D are adhered to. The standards and disciplines come alive when they're executed daily.

• • •

C.

Personal Marketing Resumes (Sales)

The Personal Marketing Resume is the single most effective marketing tool a salesperson can use. When formulated correctly, you are carefully explaining all the ways in which your customers will benefit when they do business with you. The more special and unique these added values are, the more of a positive effect they will have. The PMR gives you a very special identity.

The PMR is also the department leader's greatest assurance that the new culture is being implemented. It is not only a great position tool, it makes the sales person accountable to perform these values. If you tell people that this is what they can expect from you, you better do it. When leaders conduct their weekly in field coaching visits with their sales rep, they will know very quickly the effect of the resume.

The PMR is formulated by reviewing your added values and understanding your customer's needs. The department leader has already created theirs and should serve as the facilitator in this exercise. In a team environment, each salesperson should present their resume to the team and feel comfortable before using it in the field.

Create Loyal Customers in an Unloyal World

In 1993 I was hired by Copytronics, a Minolta copier dealer with four locations in Florida, to conduct sales training. That is where I met two great sales representatives- Alan Peck and Todd Boren. They were both outstanding sales professionals and training them was a joy for me. They worked out of the Orlando Florida office.

When I first started my training session, unbeknownst to me, they were very skeptical. In the past, they hired trainers that were neither credible nor effective. They indicated to me that the prior trainers used mundane techniques out of a book. They sat in front and admitted to me later, that they were prepared to be confrontational and take issue with my training techniques.

When the first day was completed, they came up to me and said that the sales training was the best they had ever experienced. I was very pleased, and once I found out their sales history was even more delighted. Both had great reputations in sales, and Alan Peck was nationally recognized.

Alan was the number one Minolta copier sales rep in the USA. Every year for nine consecutive years, he sold more Minolta copiers than anyone in the country. To recognize his outstanding performance, Copytronics would lease him a new BMW every year. To this day Alan is the finest salesperson I have ever trained. He is a great added value problem solver and is dedicated to helping all his clients succeed.

To emphasize this point, I want to tell you of an in field coaching visit I had with him. This visit was early in my consulting with Copytronics, and before we had formulated personal marketing resumes. The sales team PMR session was forth coming. Alan had scheduled a new call with a beer distributorship, whose lease was expiring with their current copier company, and I asked if I could accompany him. Alan was not aware that Copytronics had a not so favorable past with the perspective customer, and we found out how unfavorable it was very quickly into the meeting.

We were greeted by a department manager, and she told us that she did not think Minolta copiers were quality copiers and explained her reasoning. Three years ago a representative from Copytronics came in with a demo Minolta copier and tried to demonstrate the benefits of the copier. During the demonstration, the Minolta copier broke down. The sales rep could not get the copier to work and were not happy when they were asked to leave. Besides she stated that she loved her Cannon copier and planned on renewing her contract with them. She even commented on the favorable service that she was receiving.

When confronted with this type of situation, most sales reps would say thank you for your time and leave- but not Alan Peck. Alan asked her one very important question. Has your Cannon copier ever broke down at an inappropriate time and prevented you from meeting an important deadline?

She very passionately answered him by saying yes and went on to explain that it happened recently, and she had tried to fix the copier herself because her deadline was so important, with no results. She also explained that she did not blame Cannon because it states very clearly in its contract that their service department requires a specific amount of time to react when servicing an account.

Alan said to her that his company's service contract states the same, but if this ever happens when you are doing business with me, call me, not my service department, and I will pick you up and bring you to our offices. Alan went on to say that Copytronics has access to fifty plus copiers and along with his staff will complete the job. He said all copiers can breakdown and most copiers including Cannon and Minolta are of similar quality, the only difference between the two is making sure the customer is super served during a crisis. We talked for a time, and her attitude towards us had greatly improved when we left.

A couple of weeks later, he called me to inform me that he just signed the beer distributer that we previously visited to a $26,000 contract. I was elated and wanted her number to call her and thank her for the business. I called, I introduced myself, and thanked her for using Copytronics. She told me she was not buying Copytronics, she was buying Alan Peck. She told me that it was very reassuring to have someone like Alan as her trusted advisor.

Sales Training

Alan's career has continued to prosper after being lured away from Copytronics. Alan is presently Executive Vice President of Pinnacle Financial Group and still effectively uses his resume. Here is a copy of that resume:

Alan D. Peck - Wealth Management Advisor

My Mission

To advise, communicate, deliver and execute on your financial objectives for today and the future. This means to me, that I will tirelessly strive to do my very best to provide the smartest options to accomplish your financial goals, deliver results, and help your estate maintain positive growth.

My Strengths

Part of local, independent, boutique investment firm
One-on-one relationships with my clients
Limited, select clientele
No wirehouse mentality — I focus on you
Part of your personal investment team

My Firm's Strengths

PFG is a NASD Broker Dealer
Unblemished track record as a financial advisor
3 Innovative investment services, tailored to fit you, including 401(k), private placement, and capital raises
Viable relationships with world class money managers
Deep bench of financial services

Create Loyal Customers in an Unloyal World

My Commitment
To always remain professional, ethical, and loyal
To invest the time necessary to understand your individual investment goals
Available to you anytime, in the capacity you desire
Understanding and setting mutual expectations based on realistic goals and objectives
Putting YOUR best interests FIRST

My Vision
    To develop a life-long relationship based on results and accomplishment
    Advising you with respect and integrity in an unconditional, customized manner supported by independent advice and counsel.
    Making my professional dedication to you unparalleled in the financial investment community

If I am able to please you with my services and investment performance, I would enjoy being able to help your friends and family who may be able to use my services. Similar to other businesses my growth and success are achieved primarily through the referrals of my delighted customers.

I appreciate the opportunity to earn your business.

PFG Headquarters
1030 N. Orange Ave, Suite 210
Orlando, Florida 32801
Tel. 407.622.8118
Fax. 407. 622.8119
www.TheWealthCo.com

Bermuda Office
Hamilton, Bermuda
Tel. 441.295.1593
Direct. 441.505.4168

Sales Training

Everything that Alan professes he does and his success is a testament to his efforts. The PMR is only as good as the individual's commitment to them.

• • •

D.

Client Needs Analysis (Sales)

Information is a very important element in a customer focused culture. The effective customer focused sales professional solves their customer's problems, as we discussed in the previous section of this chapter regarding Alan Peck. Information generates thought and thought stimulate ideas. Customer focused sales professionals sell recommendations not product and price, and that is why they are so valuable to their clients. I have tried to stress this point throughout my book.

Information gathering and logging that information is a top priority in this process. Knowing what information is beneficial will involve input from the entire sales team. Your Client Needs Analysis (CNA) will be developed in the office not in the field. A facilitator will be chosen by the group, and the process will begin.

Because you and your team are customer focused, your CNA will be extensive. You are trying to identify needs that are preventing your client from growing their business. Some of these areas will not relate to your product. But many areas of the customers concerns will pertain to your philosophy. Such as: there is a decrease in sales production, and our company is finding it difficult to compete with our competitors on product and price. Your customers may need help in finding answers to these questions and more. These are questions your company has already faced, so the answers are at hand.

Once gathered your ability to understand the clients situation is enhanced greatly. Since you come from a customer focused culture, you can start weekly client strategic problem solving meetings. These meetings will involve the clients and the sales team. The sales person, who is the facilitator, will be the one who brings in the client. The sessions will conclude with a defined action plan. These meetings can be held in the client's office or your office. They should always have a prior approved defined agenda with a start and end time. There should be a rule of no interruptions. Never any cell phones!

I have included an example of a CNA for your perusal. It is to stimulate thought. It may not apply to your business but can be expanded upon. Some of the questions on your CNA should pertain to your new customer focused culture for two reasons. First, you want to help your customers business grow, and converting them to a sales driven customer focused environment will help to do that. Second, you want your customer to depend on you and your expertise, and no other rep will have you or your team's expertise in this area.

Please review the enclosed CNA.

<u>Sales Training</u>

"I WILL NEVER ASK FOR YOUR BUSINESS UNLESS I CAN HELP IMPROVE YOUR BUSINESS"

Briefly describe your business.

COMPANY PHILOSOPHY

1. What is your company's #1 job priority?

2. Do you have a company mission statement?

   A. If yes, who formulated the statement?

   B. Can everyone in your company recite your statement?

   C. Is it driven by your customers?

   D. Define your customers:

      1.
      2.
      3.

3. Do your managers understand their #1 job priority?

    A.   Is it clearly defined?

4. Are your managers empowered to make decisions?

5. Are your employees empowered to make client decisions?

    A.   What does employee empowerment mean to you?

Comments:

COMPETITIVE ANALYSIS

1. List your 3 major competitors.

2. Do you have a defined competitive edge?

3. Versus your major competitor, how do you rate in these 3 areas?

   A. Share of dollars

   B. Product or services rendered

   C. Employee training (expertise)

4. What are your company's major strengths?

   A. Major weaknesses?

5. What are your competitor's major strengths?

   A. Major weaknesses?

Comments:

MARKETING INFORMATION

1. Who is your desired target?

    Age (heavy user)

    Sex

    Income

    Location

    Life Style characteristics

    Socio-economic

2. What are your target's principle buying considerations?

    1.
    2.
    3.

3. How is your company's philosophy conveyed to your target?

    Radio   Billboards

    TV   Trades

    Newspaper   Other

Sales Training

4. Is the majority of your advertising tactical or strategic? (Please give an example of your most recent ads)

5. Are you the market leader in your target's mind?

Comments:

SELLING PHILOSOPHY

1. Do you have a Client Needs Analysis form?
   (If yes, please show example.)

2. Does your CNA have only product-related questions?

3. Do your sales people share the CNA with other departments before making client recommendations?

4. After CNA sessions, do your sales people give their clients a choice or specific recommendation?

5. Do your sales representatives understand the following about their clients?

   > Target
   > Buying cycle
   > Buying modes
   > Target's buying consideration
   > Buying influences

6. Is it required that your sales reps keep updated, detailed client files?

7. Do you prioritize all your accounts (strategic account list management)?

Sales Training

8. Is new business development important to your company's success?

    A. On a yearly basis, what percentage of your total business is new?

9. Do you have in place a new account development system?

10. A. Are your sales people trained in delighting customers?

    B. Are they required to know their mission statement?

    C. Do they have a list of added values important in creating customer relationships?

    D. Do they have a list of standards and disciplines important in creating delighted customers?

    E. Do they have Personal Marketing Resumes?

11. How do your sales reps position themselves versus competitors?

12. Sales department's greatest strengths? Weaknesses?

13. Projections:

    A. Are they mandatory?

    B. Is an action plan submitted with projections?

    C. Who determines yearly projections (employees, manager or both)?

    D. Are projections formulated account by account?

Comments:

MANAGEMENT SECTION

1. Do your managers submit departmental plans yearly?

2. Do your managers have written employee evaluations?

    If yes, how many times per year?

3. Do your managers have a job description?

    If yes, are supervisory and functional duties separated?

4. What are your managers' most important priorities?

5. Do your managers empower their employees?

6. What are your managers' greatest challenges this year?

Comments:

CLIENT EXPECTATIONS

1. If you hire a consultant to help you improve your business what improvements are you expecting?

Comments:

Sales Training

ADDITIONAL QUESTIONS

1. What is the #1 reason for your company's success?

2. Where are your greatest growth opportunities?

3. Which department is your biggest money maker?

4. Do you have customer focus group sessions with staff & clients?

5. If there was one thing about your business that — if more people knew about it — could bring you more business, what would that one thing be?

Comments:

The questions on my CNA are focused on my client's success. They are also questions that I can only answer or facilitate the answers, which automatically makes me a valuable resource. Your CNA must be accompanied by strategic problem solving meetings. Your job is to identify the problem your goal is to solve it. The answers to these questions are gathered over a period of time and logged in your CNA file for future reference.

• • •

E.

Techniques and Terminology

In this section of the sales training, we are going to define correct sales techniques and terminology needed in becoming a successful sales professional. In the beginning of my book, I said that I could train anyone in sales and I still feel that way. Excelling in sales takes time, focus and effort.

If your goal is always focused on helping each of your customers obtain success, you are half way there. That is what I describe as being a sales driven individual. If you learn some very basic techniques and continue to fine tune those skills, you can enjoy a successful sales career.

Doing the little things right is the first step in your development. We formulated some basic standards & disciplines previously in this chapter. On a completed list, we would have items such as: proper attire, punctuality and always having a pen and pad on each call. These items are as basic as it gets, yet it demonstrates a professional demeanor.

In this chapter, we are going to discuss sales techniques and terminology that are also basic, but very important to know. In developing my system, I was introduced to many sales elements, and I kept the ones that I found to be important and discarded the rest. The first term I am going to explain is Buying Modes.

1. Buying Modes:

Buying mode describes the customers need. Are they a viable candidate that you should spend time with? One of the worst things you can do as a salesperson is waste your time on the wrong account. It is discouraging and time consuming.

The four buying modes are Over Confident, Even Keel, Growth and Trouble.

1. **Over Confident**- A client that is over confident thinks their business situation is better than it may be and has no interest in your product. Wasting a lot of your valuable time trying to convince them other wise may be painful for you and them. If they remain in this mode, they are not a prospect.

2. **Even Keel**- Someone who is even keel is not seeking advice, because they are content in their current situation. Again don't waste your time.

3. **Growth**- Is a potential client to pursue. They want to expand their business and are willing to listen to anyone that can give them helpful advice. They are in

need of a problem solver. They are candidates for a complete CNA and strategic planning sessions.

4. **Trouble**- When a company is in a trouble mode they need problem solving advice. They are also a potential customer that warrants your time and attention. Make sure they are solvent.

2. Buying Cycle

The next element to discuss is Buying Cycle. A Buying Cycle is when your potential prospect is most likely to buy your services. I told you about Alan Peck earlier and his call on a beer distributorship. He knew that the beer distributor's copier lease was expiring soon. It was a three year lease, and that is why he pursued them. Alan knew their buying cycle. If Alan had gone in too early, the beer distributorship could not have contracted with his company, even if they wanted to. Make sure you know your clients and potential clients buying cycle. It is something you can include in your CNA. In fact all of these techniques can be included in the CNA.

3. Buying Influences

There are four buying influences in the complex sale, and they are: the Economic Buyer,

User Buyer, Technical Buyer and Coach and you should know all of them. Your sale depends on it. This is real important, your sales growth will be greatly affected.

1. **Economic Buyer (EB)** Is the person that releases the funds. They are very high up in the corporate chain, and making contact with them is difficult. They want to solve the problem and are very important to the customer focused rep. They want the problem solved, but unfortunately we do not have access to them (All is not lost read on).

2. **User Buyer (UB)** benefits from the funds released. For example, if the owner (EB) of a car dealership wants to increase car sales and releases funds for an advertising campaign enabling the sales manager to make their projections, the sales manager is classified as the user buyer, because they benefit from the funds released.

3. **Technical Buyer (TB)** is the gate keeper. They are only interested in product and price; in fact, they usually cannot go beyond those specific guidelines. They are usually the people that most sales people have to interact with. The problem is that they are price sensitive only,

and a problem solving sales rep is of little interest to them.

4. **The Coach** is someone that has access and credibility with the buying influences, and because you have a strong relationship with them, they want you to win. They may work within the organization and even be one of the buying influences. They are the key to your success because of their ability to access the other buying influences.

Understanding the buying influences is the key to a successful customer focused rep. The definition of the complex sale is that there is more than one decision maker. That is why you can lose out on a sale that you thought was in the bag. Developing a coach in every complex sale is very important to completing the sale.
The technical buyer is there to level the playing field in favor of the client. They are very price sensitive and do not care about your problem solving skills. The other buying influences may but without the coach, you may never be able to interact with them personally.

4. CNA versus Budget

Most sales people try to determine their client's budget before they create their proposal. I train the opposite. In my training sessions, I tell my sales reps to do a thorough CNA before trying to sell anything. When a CNA is done correctly, you should be able to determine the needs of your customer. Your proposal should be focused on solving the customer's problem by eliminating the need. What the client has budgeted may not be enough to fix the problem. As a customer focused professional, your goal is to help your clients achieve success.

An example: If you were buying a house, you would sit down with your real estate salesperson and discuss your needs. You would let them know the area you wanted, the school district, and the size and style of the house. You would also tell them what you wanted to spend. They would conduct a CNA.

After doing so, the real estate salesperson may only have two choices, to try to accommodate your life style needs and show you how to pay for it, or put you and your family in the wrong house and neighborhood to meet your budget.

If they did the latter, and put you in the wrong house to meet your budget, they are not customer focused. Their job is to show you how to get the home of your dreams, and help you pay for it with their real estate insight. They should sit down with you and review your expenses, and introduce you to their contacts at various lending institutions etc.

A professional customer focused sales person should assist you in any way they can to assure your total satisfaction. That is the definition of a customer focused sales professional.

5. Recommendation versus Choice

Customer focused sales professionals sell ideas not product. In the beginning of my book, we discussed the importance of having an individual identity, and described it as a defined Competitive Edge Identity. When a sales rep tells their client to choose instead of making a recommendation, it is like a doctor that tells their patient to pick their cure after they examine them. It compromises the doctor and requires the patient to be the expert.

A professional customer focused rep is in charge of the sale when they make well thought out recommendations. I was conducting a sales seminar for a real estate company and was challenged after telling them that professional sales reps always make recommendations and never let their clients choose. In fact, I stated that showing a lot of houses confuses the customer and compromises their expertise. They should show them three houses and recommend one.

A very successful real estate women really voiced her disapproval about making a recommendation. She said that the customer knew best and should be the only one that is qualified to make the final decision on which house is the right house. I told her that the client always makes the final decision, but after doing a CNA, you should lead them to the correct decision by making a recommendation. She disagreed and said that the client was more qualified than her to make their own recommendation, and the group agreed.

So I asked her how many homes she had sold in the last year, and she said 44. I asked her if I could assume that she had also shown hundreds of homes during that same period of time and she replied at least. So I continued by asking her how many homes would someone traditionally buy from her in a year, and she said one. I said you sold 44 homes and showed hundreds more, and your clients traditionally buy one home, and that makes the client more qualified in home buying than you? The group went silent.

It is faster and easier to sell the wrong product. It does not require any effort or professionalism. The product focused sales person does not have to live with the wrong product after the sale. Customer Focused Professional sales people make qualified recommendations based on their expertise because their focus is to meet and exceed their client's needs.

6. Written Presentation

When submitting a written proposal, I like them short and to the point. They should identify the need and describe how you will fix the problem. I am going to give you eight necessary elements that should be included and explain the importance of each one.

1. **Title page** should include the persons name and title that the proposal is being submitted to along with your name, title and date.

2. **Objective** of the proposal should define the goal.

3. **Executive Summary** is the overview of the entire proposal without mentioning price or specific details. It's the proposal in summary form.

4. **Need** describes the specific need in detail.

5. **Problem Solving** is defining how the need/problem will be solved.

6. **Why do business with you?** Is an overview of the virtues of you and your company, and gives you a chance to present the benefits of your philosophy. When you have a customer focused philosophy, it allows you a forum to describe it.

7. **Fees/investment** should be described on this page as a business investment, if the proposal is constructed properly.

8. **References** should always be included in every proposal. It gives you great credibility when a client sings your praises. When you have to say how good you are that is bragging, but when a client speaks highly of you that's an important endorsement.

A proposal from a customer focused professional should help the client understand that their problem will be solved, because they are dealing with problem solvers.

7. Creative Problem Solving Session (Sales)

Now that the sales training elements have been completed, they must be constantly reviewed to assure execution. The department leader should schedule weekly strategic meetings to review all the elements of the system. It will build team unity and assure that everyone is on the same page.

These creative problem solving sessions are for the sales team only, and are in lieu of your client strategic meetings. The team should be involved in helping each other improve their skills. That is the definition of team. To have a customer focused culture is to have unity within.

Sales Training

I explained early in my book that leadership meant employee development. These creative problem solving meetings with clients and employees are designed to do that. Leaders should never stop training their people.

• • •

F.

Strategic Account List Management

When your company changes to a customer focused selling philosophy, time becomes of the essence. A professional customer focused sales representative becomes a valuable resource to their clients by providing them many important added values, like those we have already described. It would be impossible to provide every client on your list all of these services. Time would not allow it.

For instance, time will not allow you to conduct a complete CNA with every client and still be productive. If you spend an equal amount of time with every client, you will fail in sales. You must prioritize your clients as to their growth potential in order to maximize your growth, as well as your client's growth. All clients do not deserve the same amount of attention, so which clients deserve the most time?

Strategic account list management categorizes accounts into four areas: Key, Target, Secondary and Extra. They are as follows:

Key accounts are 20% of the clients that provide 80% of your total billing revenue. They are your largest accounts and should receive all your added value services. You should continually gather information through a CNA to find areas where you can assist them. You should conduct marketing models and invite all the buying influences to participate. Your time will be well spent assisting your key accounts in their growth potential.

Previously we stated that Willie Sutton said that he robbed banks, "because that's where the money is." Taking Willie's advice professional, sales reps should immerse themselves with their Key accounts because that's where the money is. Growing your key accounts will assure your growth.

Target accounts have the dollar potential to become key accounts and must meet the ideal customer profile. My ideal customer profile consists of 3 elements Dollar Potential, Access and Credibility with the buying influences and Product Fit (I will explain each element after we finish reviewing the 4 account categories). Identifying target accounts and then converting them to key accounts is the single most important responsibility that a sales rep can do to assure continued growth. The target accounts have great potential, so they need lots of time and attention. The sales team's strategic weekly sessions should focus on their conversion. The department leader should limit each rep to no more than five target accounts at any one time.

Secondary accounts are doing business with your company, but do not have the potential to become key accounts. These accounts are important to your growth, but they should not receive too much of your time and attention because of their limited growth potential. When you interact with them or any other client, you are still there to help them succeed.

Extra accounts are non-billing accounts. Many of these accounts are new and should be continually evaluated for their potential.

All accounts on your list should be assigned one of the four categories we have just discussed. As a professional customer focused sales rep, all accounts are important and should be treated with great respect. Clients with the most potential should be given the most time and attention. That's just smart time management.

1. Ideal Customer Profile

Dollar Potential means those client accounts that represent huge potential revenue sources for the sales rep and company. They have the capability to become key accounts. They are obviously very important to the growth of any company, and if the dollar potential client meets the rest of the ideal customer profile, they should receive all your added value services.

Access and Credibility with the buying influences is very important in a customer focused selling system. In fact, I have always felt that this was the most important element in converting target accounts to key accounts. Before I would allow my sales reps to classify any account as a target account they had to have access and credibility with someone other than the technical buyer. I didn't care how much dollar potential a client had because without having strong relationships with the other buying influences any proposal would be premature.

I have always felt that my goal as a successful leader was to build belief with my staff in my management techniques and in our team's strategic training philosophy. Nothing builds belief more than success. I wanted each member of my team to succeed in the field by implementing the right strategies to the right people at the right time. Having access and credibility with the buying influences assures a more successful outcome and a higher closing percentage.

Product Fit means that your client needs matches your product and services. This is an easy one because as a customer focused sales rep your primary job is to assist your customers in the growth of their business. If you sell them the wrong product, as we discussed in the CNA versus Budget section of this chapter, you are not helping yourself or your client. It will damage your reputation and prevent your client's growth.

Sales Training

Some companies have more elements to the ideal customer profile. But if you focus on the three elements, we have just discussed, you will be able to help your clients succeed. Growing your key accounts is vital to your success. Converting your target to key accounts is also paramount to your growth.

Remember key accounts are currently doing business with your company and represent the top 20% in billing revenue. Your target accounts must meet the ideal customer profile to be considered a serious prospect. Both the key and target accounts are where you should be spending the majority of your time with.

• • •

CHAPTER V
Marketing

The success of any business is greatly enhanced with a comprehensive marketing effort. After creating a customer focused, corporate, leadership and sales driven philosophy, I concentrate my efforts on helping companies market that philosophy. My goal is to help companies increase its understanding of marketing by explaining the elements and techniques required in creating a successful marketing campaign.

It is obvious to any organization the importance of marketing to its desired target. Companies understands that without a comprehensive marketing effort, it is very difficult to survive in today's competitive marketplace; how to effectively do it is the question.

It is with disbelief as I watch some of the commercials on television. Many of the messages are confusing to the target audience. Some of these confusing messages may be reaching the target, but I still find them ineffective, such as: "so easy a caveman can do it." What is so easy, buying insurance? I didn't know it was difficult to buy insurance. The advertising campaign may be successful in reaching the target, but I just don't know what message they are trying to communicate. I don't like "silly" advertising anyway, unless your target is children.

Occasionally a company will experience initial success in their marketing efforts, but the same message becomes stagnant. Companies do not change the message to meet their target's changing needs. When you define your target, you should always focus on the heavy user. The heavy user is the one who will most likely buy your goods and services.

In the broadcasting business, most stations that sell advertising communicate its station's strengths by broadly featuring its statistics regarding listenership, and this is misleading. In the first chapter, I stated that the rating statistics were flawed because the numbers were weighted. They are also misleading because most radio sales reps will provide rating numbers in too broad of a demo group. Instead of breaking down the audience statistics as the rating services give it to them 12-17, 18-24, 25-34, 35-44, 45-54 etc. they lump these numbers together to make their stations appear more in line with their client's needs.

For instance, they will show how many people the station reaches in the 25-54 year old age group at any given time period, because that is the age group that many advertisers try to reach. This is misleading because not only are the numbers weighted, but if any station has a lot of 25 year old listeners at a giving time, they have very few 54 year olds listening in that same time period.

Marketing

Most 25 and 54 years olds have little in common with each other, but if a station has enough younger listeners, for example, it will allow them to inflate the overall numbers. Especially if they think those numbers are of interest to you. For example, if a 25 year old uses a product a 54 year old will probably not use the same product and vice versa. The marketing techniques that we will discuss in this chapter take all of that into consideration and I will show you a better way to market your business.

In this chapter we are going to introduce and demonstrate the benefits of a marketing model. The marketing model will be very beneficial to your company's marketing efforts because it narrowly defines your target by focusing only on the heavy user. The heavy user, as we briefly alluded to earlier, is your real target-the people most interested in your goods and services.

I am also going to show you three actual "positioning statements" that I have developed for various companies. These statements clearly and effectively communicate the clients business to its target. I am only going to show you three statements from diverse clients in order to illustrate that a positioning statement can be used by any business effectively. When that is completed, I will introduce strategic and tactical marketing campaigns and how to use them.

• • •

A.

Marketing Model / Define Product

1. Target
- Tight age demo-based on heavy user
- Sex: percentage male vs. female
- Income: define targets income
- Location: where do they live?
- Soc-Eco: work status
- Lifestyle: homeowners, renter, family, single, # cars etc.

2. Product
- **K**ey **B**uying **C**onsideration of target.
- What attracts target to product?

3. Competitive Analysis
- Which company currently owns the key buying consideration in the targets mind? If some else owns the position we need to reposition them.

4. Position (Formulating a Positioning Statement)
- Unique - or enhanced to be unique
- Credible - must deliver on message
- KBC - must be included in statement (key buying consideration)

5. **Promotion**
   - Tactical campaign – price, item and dated offer (reason to respond)
   - Strategic campaign - advertising with testimonials and benefits of business, signage, brochures.

When I first was introduced to the marketing model, I was very intrigued because I knew the broad demo groups that I was trained to sell had many flaws. The target section of the marketing model was very narrow regarding the desired targets age and instantly made sense to me. It was diametrically opposed to the media's ratings service ideology and therefore credible.

In order to be successful in a marketing campaign, it is extremely important to know the psychographics of your target. For instance, if your product was targeted to 45-54 year old men, with an average income of $250,000, and their key buying consideration was luxury and performance in an automobile you would not advertise on a country or rock radio station no matter what there 45-54 year old numbers indicated. These formats attract an audience whose average income is too low, and therefore they will have a different key buying consideration when car shopping. In other words, they are clearly not the target yet they meet the age requirement.

That's why advertising can be so confusing. Before you are ready to spend your hard earn dol-

Marketing

lars on a marketing campaign I recommend that you completely understand your narrow target, their key buying consideration, and the current market leader. Then create a positioning statement. When you have completed this exercise, you are ready to promote your business.

• • •

B.

Positioning Statement

Creating a positioning statement will give your company an important identity in your desired targets mind. If you are diligent and follow the process that I just demonstrated, you will take your advertising campaigns to a new level.

I discovered a couple of things early in my marketing career. Marketing a product successfully is not as much about the product, as it is about the target's perceptions of the product. If the target thinks one product is better than another that is what sells that product, and it does not matter if it is better. The product leader just communicates the message more effectively. That's why the creation of a positioning statement based on the key buying considerations of the target is effective.

When I was general sales manager my sales rep and I visited a tree nursery that was advertising with our radio station. Its business was successful because they had a quality product. Even though business was good, they had a reputation of being priced higher than its competitors and wanted some help in changing the buyer's perception to increase its market share.

We did a marketing model and found out that the two key buying considerations of the target were quality and price. The nursery had a great reputation for quality, but they were perceived to have high prices. The company's positioning statement at the time was "landscaping that speaks for itself." I though the statement effectively addressed the quality concerns of the target, but did not address the price objection.

As I stated earlier in the actual marketing model (above), a positioning statement must be unique or enhanced in such a way to be unique. It must be credible by delivering on the message and based on the key buying consideration of the target. So to insure credibility, we had to get the nursery's competitors price sheet and compared prices, because we did not want to claim they were competitively priced if they weren't. After examination, we found them to be close enough in price to continue the exercise.

Our goal was to create an effective positioning statement that overcame the price objection, while maintaining their reputation for quality. The statement we formulated was as follows: **"You know our quality you'll be surprised by our prices."** It is a little longer than I like, but we repositioned our client effectively versus its competitors and target, regarding price.

Positioning Statements are very effective to a business in helping them communicate the message to its target. To continue to demonstrate my

Marketing

point, I am going to mention two other companies I have helped with positioning statements: Dourdas Financial and Dattoli Cancer Research Center.

Peter Dourdas owns a financial company with offices in Syracuse, New York and New York City, and does financial planning for many clients. Peter is very successful. Many of his current and perspective clients have large estates, and he wanted to communicate to them that he was qualified to meet their needs. When I completed the marketing model, I discovered two key buying considerations for his target. They needed someone they trusted to handle their money, and they wanted a company large enough to take advantage of financial opportunities. The positioning statement that I created: **"Integrity with Resources"** addresses the two key buying considerations of the target, and therefore, was very effective. He stills uses it today.

Another positioning statement I created was for a very capable doctor in Sarasota, Florida. The name of his clinic is Dattoli Cancer Research Center where I was a patient for prostate cancer. Dr. Dattoli has a great staff and was very instrumental in my complete recovery.

Since I was the target, I decided to create a positioning statement for the clinic and conducted my own marketing model. I contemplated my reasons for choosing Dr. Dattoli's treatment that specializes in radiation therapy over other doctors who specialized in other various treatments.

When I was doing my research, I found that Dr. Dattoli's prostate cancer survival rate was over ninety percent, and they treated all types of patients-some patients that other doctors thought were hopeless. Survival was my key buying consideration, and I felt that it was probably the same for most of his patients. So I proceeded to create a positioning statement focusing on survival. The statement that I created, **Dedicated to Life** was very well received by Dr. Dattoli and his staff. The statement accomplishes its goal, because it will positively influence most patients and help them in the decision making process.

These fore mentioned positioning statements hit the target between the eyes, and that is the goal because every target has a bulls-eye. You just have to know how to find it. Narrow the target, establish the key buying consideration, and then effectively position the product in your target's mind. When you do this, you are ready for the promotional elements of the marketing model.

• • •

C.

Strategic & Tactical Campaigns

Promoting a product without going through the process we just discussed is the equivalent of throwing your money away, and no one has enough money to do that. Understanding your target by narrowly defining the heavy user is the first element in creating a successful marketing campaign. Finding out your targets key buying consideration is the next element needed, and creating a position statement is the final element of the process. All of these elements should be completed before trying to promote your product.

The process is necessary to assure success. It is possible that a strong customer focused positioning statement may be the essence of your entire marketing campaign. To illustrate this, I will use the Dourdas Financial positioning statement as an example. Integrity with Resources could be the major theme of a thirty or sixty second radio or television commercial by expanding on the message. It could also be made into a print ad, because it communicates to the customer their most important buying considerations.

Strategic Campaigns communicate a message that your company is solid and gives the target specific examples. Many financial institutions use these techniques to assure its target that they are reliable and trustworthy. You can effectively advertise a strategic campaign on television, in brochures, in business publications, and even using signage in strategically positioned venues. On signage the name and positioning statement could be very effective at communicating your message in very few words. I do not feel that strategic campaigns are as effective on radio, because radio needs frequency and a call to action to be effective.

Tactical Campaigns are different and need to employ a different strategy. The tactical campaign is a call to action with a dated offer and features price and item. It is sales driven, and can be used very effectively on radio, television or print.

When used on radio, it is effective because radio is a reach and frequency medium. The listener's come in and out of the format, because many of them are mobile and are on the run. The vast majority do not listen for long periods of time. Tactical campaigns are a call to action, and since the radio listener comes in and out of the format, I recommend that you schedule your ads vertically rather than horizontally.

That means you schedule as many commercials to run each day till the schedule runs out. As an example if you purchase twenty commercials, schedule them over two days rather than running them Monday through Sunday. That's because radio as I said earlier is a reach and frequency medium. You

Marketing

not only have to reach your target, but you have to make many impressions on them to be effective.

Television on the other hand has a different type of audience. Those that watch television view for longer periods of time, because they watch programs. Many are at home, and they are immobile. Tactical campaigns can be effective on television, but instead of buying a vertical schedule, you would buy programs, and I recommend that you buy multiple spots per program, especially on those programs that attract your target.

When using print to run a tactical campaign, you can buy a section of the newspaper that your target is most likely to read. For example, the sport section, if you are trying to attract a male target that has an interest in sports, or the financial section, if your target is an investor. The newspaper can be very effective, because you can list the price and items, and include coupons.

Tactical campaigns are designed to move product. Remember the tactical ad includes price and item, a dated offer, and a reason to respond. Price and item means that it is sales driven, a dated offer means that the target has to respond quickly to take advantage of the offer. Tactical campaigns create urgency, which forces the target to respond, and that is always beneficial to the advertiser.

• • •

Job Descriptions

Job descriptions that are also evaluation forms help emphasis and monitor customer focused job responsibilities for each employee. When completed the job description will even serve as a valuable interviewing guide. Department Leaders and their employees will formulate the job description. Leaders will conduct 3- 6 month evaluations.

JOB DESCRIPTION/EVALUATION FORM

    ( ) Supervisor
    ( ) Self

Scale
    1. Excellent
    2. Good
    3. Average
    4. Below Average
    5. Unsatisfactory

Job Title _____

Name _____

Supervisor/Title and Name _____

Department _____

Administrative

1. PURPOSE

- Department Specific Mission:
- Leadership Statement - To build a partnership with you, to assist you in achieving your business goals through understanding specific needs, solving problems, and providing timely *service...Enthusiastically.*

2. JOB DUTIES (Leader's prioritize all supervisory duties from most important to least important)

SUPERVISORY

-( )

-( )

-( )

-( )

-( )

-( )

Create Loyal Customers in an Unloyal World

-( )

-( )

-( )

-( )

COMMENTS: _____
_____
_____

As you will notice I have separated supervisory duties from non supervisory or functional duties. This is very important because when leaders stop leading it is usually a direct result of having too many non supervisory duties and that must be corrected. With our job description/evaluation form this problem will be very easy to identify and correct.

Administrative

FUNCTIONAL DUTIES

( )

( )

( )

( )

( )

( )

( )

( )

( )

( )

COMMENTS: _____

_____

_____

_____

RELATIONSHIPS

To understand who our customers are

- Vendors
- Peers
- Clients

And to accommodate their concerns

( )   To maintain an open line of communication with management and all employees

( )   To conduct business in an honest and truthful manner

( )   To deal with the staff in a professional manner showing courtesy and respect

( )   To give recognition for outstanding performance

( )   To constructively appraise performance for improvement

( )   To uplift and encourage the staff

( )   To provide leadership and development

Administrative

( ) To listen

( ) To respond enthusiastically with creative solutions

( ) To welcome constructive appraisal from management

Comments:

3. Job Experience/Knowledge/Educational Level

Required	Desired	Explanation
_____	_____	_____
_____	_____	_____
_____	_____	_____
_____	_____	_____

4. Skills/Behavior Characteristics

**H=High Level Required   M=Moderate Required
L=Low Level Required O/NR**

Yes/No	Level Required	Category
_____	_____	1. Flexibility
_____	_____	2. Oral Communications
_____	_____	3. Written Communications
_____	_____	4. Delegation
_____	_____	5. Leadership
_____	_____	6. Initiative

Administrative

_____ _____	7.	Planning and Organizing
_____ _____	8.	Judgment
_____ _____	9.	Stress Tolerance
_____ _____	10.	Salesmanship
_____ _____	11.	Time Management
_____ _____	12.	Sensitivity
_____ _____	13.	Customer Orientation
_____ _____	14.	Analytical Skills

Comments:

_____

_____

Have your job duties/responsibilities increased or change since your last review?
Please explain:

Date _____

Employee Signature _____

Leaders Signature _____

For annual reviews only:

Salary Adjustment Recommendation:

    Effective date _____

    Leaders Approval
    _____

• • •

Departmental Plans

Departmental Plans are completed prior to the upcoming year and serve as a valuable compass for department leaders. Leaders that are given the power to lead their staff, earn that privilege by having a clear vision. Power is given to those who have a vision for growth. Here is an example. It is only an example and can be expanded upon.

Departments Vision for Growth

Department Status
1. What were your department's most significant accomplishments in the previous 12 months?
2. Describe your department's goals for the next 12 months.
3. What opportunities were lost?
4. Employee status.

Problem Areas
1. Current department concerns.
2. Recommended Solutions.
3. Future areas of concern.
4. Recommended Solutions.

Competitive Overview
1. Most significant competitors.
2. Strategy to combat a competitive attack.

Staff Development
1. Employee Evaluation.
2. Leader's development strategy for training each employee.

Employee bank
1. Define a strategy designed to continually indentify talented prospects.

Selling Philosophy
1. Define sales philosophy.
2. Describe in detail departments plan for growth.
3. Attached a line by line action plan with detailed department projections.

Date: _____ **Signature** _____

The initial departmental plan takes time to complete. After the first plan has been completed and evaluated it becomes a way of life and forces the leader of the department to have a defined strategy. This will help the department leader as well as the executives who will evaluate them to have

Administrative

a clear understanding of each department's problems, opportunities for growth and goals.

The leader of the department benefits most because it helps them to articulate a clear vision for growth and a structured strategy to succeed. As the famous Chinese general Sun Tzu once said "the general who wins in battle makes many calculations in his temple before the battle is fought."

Your plans and strategy assures victory.

• • •

Create Loyal Customers in an Unloyal World

Training Workbook

My workbook is designed to reinforce my book **How to Create Loyal Customers in an Unloyal World**. It will assist department leaders in their training by reinforcing the new culture to current employees and serve as a valuable guide in training new employees. The training workbook is a clear concise way to help you achieve the highest level of performance.

Workbook

Introduction

Your training will be very extensive and very much focused on the customer. When completed you will understand "How to Create Loyal Customers in an Unloyal World." You will understand the importance of a well defined Mission Statement. Your new customer focused corporate training will explain the importance of such things as a client needs analysis's, added values and personal marketing resumes all needed to insure customer loyalty. These new customer focused techniques are powerful and will create a team of problem solving entrepreneurs.

The evaluation and implementation of my system will enable you to become very externally focused and therefore able to help your

Administrative

clients at all levels from store level to marketing needs. When executed properly, you will never again be limited to product and price comparisons. You will truly become an added value resource.

• • •

TABLE OF CONTENTS

1. **CULTURAL SECTION**   **161**

2. **LEADERSHIP SECTION**   **163**

3. **SALES TRAINING**   **166**

4. **COMPETIVE ANALYSIS**   **168**

5. **MARKETING**   **169**

...

CORPORATE CULTURE:

Changing your culture from a product oriented environment to a customer focused environment is the single most important thing a company can do. It will help build a team spirit and assures employee participation. When each employee understands their role in this philosophy it will lead to a successful outcome internally and externally.

Your corporate culture will never be outdated as long as you understand your client's needs and solve their problems. The following section is a review of everything we have read and can be used to help bring new employees up to speed very quickly.

What is your defined Mission Statement?

Who and what determines your strategy?

Name 3 ways in which you have demonstrated that you are customer focused.

What is your unique competitive advantage?

Name 3 ways you have separated yourself from your competitors.

Why are your added values so important to your success?

Why are your added values important to your customer?

Why are good standards and discipline important?

Name 3 standards and disciplines that you feel have been helpful in building loyalty.

What is the value of a Personal Marketing Resume?

• • •

Administrative

LEADERSHIP:

A Leaders ability to understand and implement the training is a testament to their ability to lead. Their staff's ability to properly execute the customer focused sales philosophy is the standard by which they should be judged. It is the key ingredient to the corporation's success.

Are you empowered to run your department and make employee decisions?

Prioritize your leadership duties from most important to least.

What does employee development mean to you?

Give an example of how you have given empowerment.

Describe your current employee training system.

Do your employees have an open line of communications with you?

Do you use your job descriptions as employee evaluation forms? How often are your employees evaluated?

When monitoring your employees on their ability to properly execute the customer focused philosophy-what's been their biggest obstacles?

Name ways you encourage a team philosophy. Is it successful?

How and when do you give employee recognition?

How would you grade yourself on your ability to recognize good performance?

Do you discipline non performance? Give examples.

Do you have an itinerary for every meeting?

What are potential problem areas for your department?

What strategies are you formulating to overcome these problems?

What is the single biggest challenge for you and your department?

Do you have a recruitment strategy if a valuable employee unexpectedly leaves the company?

Administrative

With the ever changing technology and economic conditions in your business and marketplace, what is your prognosis for the upcoming year?

Is it required that your sales reps keep updated client information?

Can all your employees recite their mission statement? Do you consistently review how they live it with their client's and peers?

Can you recite your leadership statement?

On a scale from 1-10 where is your staff in delighting their customers?

Give examples of how your staff effectively positions themselves versus their competitors.

Do you have in field visits with each sales rep on a consistent basis? How many visits per rep?

Do you have weekly strategic problem solving meetings with clients? With staff?

• • •

SALES TRAINING:

CLIENT NEEDS ANALYSIS:

What is the importance of a CNA?

What are some of your sources, beside the client for gathering information?

What information is most important?

SELLING SKILLS:

Name and explain the 4 buying modes.

Which are the most likely prospects?

Name the 4 buying influences.

Which buying influence is most interested in your problem solving skills?

Why is it important to establish access and credibility with the economic buyer?

Why is the coach, so important to the customer focused sale rep?

How do you develop your coach?

Administrative

Explain the clients buying cycle and its importance.

Identify the problem that seems to most often prevent a successful outcome.

How does emphasizing your client's budget prevent you from a successful outcome?

Why do you always give a recommendation and not a choice when selling your product?

What mode is your sales team in: creating demand or managing demand?

What objections do you find most difficult to overcome?

· · ·

COMPETITIVE ANALYSIS

List your major competitors.

Describe each competitors selling philosophy.

Describe how you sell against their philosophy.

What are the strengths of your major competitor? Weaknesses? Selling techniques?

Identify people within your competitor's organization that you feel are formidable.

What strategy has your department formulated to overcome competitor attacks?

• • •

___Administrative___

MARKETING

How do you position yourself versus your competitors with clients?

Are you considered a problem solving resource with your clients? Please explain.

Have you conducted marketing model sessions with any of your clients? If so, were they effective?

Have you helped your clients create a positioning statement?

Have you introduced your most important clients to your customer focused philosophy?

Have you tried to help them identify their corporate philosophy?

Have you explain the different ways to market a product?

What is a tactical marketing campaign?

What is a strategic marketing campaign?

Do you always have a written itinerary for every client meeting?

Do you formulate an action plan after meeting with clients?

You have just completed your corporate workbook. The workbook has been designed to be a refresher for employees that helped create the system. It can also be used in the training of new employees. The workbook insures focus and focus insures proper execution.

Your training is complete with me but you should never stop training in a customer focused organization. I have included in the client quote section, in the back of the book, a few of the individuals that I was fortunate enough to train. To eliminate any confusion I have also included a definition of terms page at the end of the book.

I wish all of you great success, always.

• • •

Epilogue

You have just read my book **Create Loyal Customers in an Unloyal World,** and I hope you enjoyed it. Every element of my customer focused, leadership, sales, and marketing system, **Step2 Training System**, has been included. It has been field tested for its effectiveness. Those that have been trained in my system are very enthusiastic with the long term results. Read the quotes from a few of my clients in the back section of the book.

For many years, I have helped companies create a customer focused environment that enabled them to become more successful in business. I feel very strongly that any company that follows the elements that I have presented in my book will greatly benefit. In my previous book, Mouth Off, I discussed some of the same topics but did not give a detailed description of every element found in my Step2 Training System.

This book is different because it is a "how to" book and gives all the elements needed in creating this culture. I presented each element in the exact order to be implemented. It is most important that you are committed to changing from a product and price focus to a real customer focused philosophy, a philosophy that is designed to delight each customer, not merely to satisfy them.

In order to accomplish this, you must include input from your entire staff in its development. Together with staff, you must create a corporate identity by narrowly defining your reason for doing business in the form of a Mission Statement. To continue to energize your identity, you must create Core Values that will give an internal direction and inspiration to your entire staff. When this process is completed, your employees will feel a sense of pride and a renewed commitment to the company. Because it is employee driven, this pride will also start to build a team spirit.

A company will eventually implode if there is employee dissention that is not reconciled. To survive, we must create a "united we stand and divided we fall mentality." To accomplish this, the next element of the system focuses on leadership. Leaders are effective when those they lead improve their skills. As we discussed, the five most important job responsibilities are to lead, to develop, to motivate, to discipline non-performance and to formulate strategies. Leaders lead people and are crucial in the development and success of this program.

To become the industry leader, a company must set the standards not follow them. To accomplish this, we discussed the importance of creating defined added values, standards and disciplines, personal marketing resumes, and structure brain-

Epilogue

storming sessions to support your new corporate philosophy. All are designed to give employees a detailed direction on how to delight their customers, all customers-internally and externally. Every element of the system is designed with employee input to assure its execution.

The power of the system is the employee design, and the assurance of success is in the monitoring by leadership. My book is an easy step by step road map to corporate success. Before you implement these elements, all employees should read and understand the process found in my book. When implemented properly, you will have a more successful company and a happier workplace.

If your corporation's entire work force buys the book, reads it and still needs assistance in the implementation of my customer focused philosophy, I will come to your business and help leadership and staff in its design. If you need assistance, my email is: cstogias@hotmail.com. Wishing you much success!

• • •

CLIENT QUOTES

"Eighteen years ago I was the # 1 top sales professional for the # 1 Minolta business equipment dealer in the USA. I then met Chuck Togias and had the privilege to hear him speak to our company and soon after that my sales literally doubled. Even better my relationships in business became stronger, my referral business jumped through the roof and I gained a mentor and a friend named Chuck Togias. I am now the executive V.P. of a successful investment firm and have been listening to and nurturing my clients for 16 years. Chuck Togias comes to work with me everyday."

> Alan D. Peck, Executive VP,
> Pinnacle Financial group

"Step2 Training Systems immediately opened my eyes to a new way of selling.... overnight I was transformed from a product oriented focus to a problem solving/solution oriented marketer. As a result, my billing increased and my relationships became stronger. The Step2 System will always be effective because the focus is to grow your clients business and as a result become a valuable resource to them."

> Donald O'Connor, GSM, TV
> Northeast market

"During my 38 year career I attended and organized dozens of training and business seminars for our company and our industry. For the last 16 years I was President & CEO for a multinational manufacturing division focusing on restructuring our sales and marketing team to meet the new challenges we were facing and will continue to face in the future. The results of the Step2 Training sessions were outstanding. Chuck Togias was endorsed 'as the best we ever had' in getting our team pointed in the right direction. The system is sophisticated yet simple in its practicality."

>William Trotman Former
>President & CEO
>Multinational Manufacturing Corporation

"Every time I have the opportunity to learn from Chuck Togias, I DO. Chuck's reputation as a dynamic and knowledgeable trainer proceeds him…wit and wisdom combined. Since being trained by the Step2 program my sales have increased by 50% despite a soft market. Step2 is simply a great sales and marketing system."

>Terri Endries
>Top biller TV sales, Northeast Market
>Voted companies top sales rep nationwide

Client Quotes

"I have used Step2 training for three different companies I have been involved with. The many benefits are as follows:

A key differentiator of this system is that instead of focusing on a feature-benefit approach, the system teaches the individual how they bring value to the client and gives them a step by step approach to make themselves an integral part of what the client is buying. This is especially critical in a commodity driven industry and takes you out of trying to compete as the low cost provider. The system forces the salesperson to be accountable for how they conduct business. This is developed in the program by each sales person committing to standards and disciplines, developing a personal marketing resume and immersing themselves into the sales equation. The program proves to be very motivational. The sales team left the training with a new sense of confidence and a new understanding on how to take their product or services to market. In some cases, it was the first time that members of the sales team believed they now brought a competitive advantage to the market place."

> Gil Korta
> Advertising Agency Executive

"For companies or individuals who have struggled to achieve their goals, Chuck Togias has a plan. Based on years of experience, the Step2 system provides a roadmap for everyone to realize their potential. Learning the system has made me far more productive inside and outside of work. I use it daily to manage my time and relationships. If you are looking to succeed, read this book and put the system to work for you."

Louis M. Centolella III, VP, Sales
Ontario Credit Corporation

• • •

Definition of terms:

Company- refers to any *small to medium size business.

Corporation- refers to *large businesses.

*Since my Step2 System's philosophy can apply to both of the above I frequently inter-change these terms.

Clients- refer to those individuals that purchase goods and services.

Customers- refers to all the company/corporation's customers: clients, peers and vendors. The term customer can also refer to clients.

Management- refers to **department heads that have not been trained in leadership techniques. Their focus is on things and not in the development of their staff.

Leaders- refer to **department heads that have been trained and are dedicated to staff training and development.

** I also purposely inter-change these terms to emphasis the importance of leadership. I want my reader to understand that managers are not necessarily leaders unless they engage in staff development.

Culture-refers to the customer focused corporate philosophy.

Philosophy refers to and is inter-changeable with corporate culture.

Rep-refers to and is an abbreviation for representative.

Target audience-refers to a narrowly defined customer group.

Product focused-refers to focusing more on product than on customer needs.

Customer focused-refers to always putting the customer's needs first.

• • •

Authors Bio:

- 1963-1965 Attended Onondaga Community College Syracuse, NY
- 1966 Parsons College Fairfield Iowa (Basketball Scholarship)
- September 1966 Drafted
- 1967-68 Military service Vietnam
- 1968 Started career in Broadcast sales
- 1971 joined NBC affiliate WSYR A/F sales staff Syracuse, New York
- 1978 became General Sales Manager 17% revenue share in a 21 station market
- 1982 sales team increased revenue share to 40%
- 1986 Revenue share 55% #1 in USA
- 1992 Created Step2 Training Systems-Corporate, Leadership, Sales and Marketing Consulting Service
- Author of 3 books: Political Correctness is BS, Mouth Off & Create Loyal Customers in an Unloyal World
- October 6, 2013 Age 70 completed 630 Chin-Ups in 2 hours 12 minutes 19 seconds World Record (not associated with Guinness)

Made in the USA
Columbia, SC
18 April 2021